THE ESTABLISHING OF BELLE VUE BY J

The Jennison Family and Adswood Strawberry Gardens

John Jennison was born in Bulwell, near Nottingham, in early 1793, one of three children (Ann, John and George Ives Jennison). The family moved to Macclesfield, where the silk industry was undergoing a period of expansion, and John Jennison senior established himself as a silk weaver with his own cottage loom. Family tradition maintains that from an early age John showed a passionate interest in botany, especially the growing of flowers. He became a gardener, but gave up this occupation rather suddenly in 1815 when there were press gangs in the area following Napoleon's escape from Elba. John fled to Stockport, where in the July of that year his father and younger brother bought 1,850 square yards of land from Ralph Jepson, yeoman. The land was located on a then unnamed road leading off Adswood Lane and was subject to an annual chief rent of £8-5s. (The road is now known as Stockholm Road and the site is occupied by a garage compound at the junction with Adswood Grove.)

It is not known how long John junior stayed in Stockport, and he later returned to Macclesfield, where he probably adopted his father's trade of silk weaver. However, a house was erected on the plot of land in 1815 and it was here that John returned following the death of his father in December 1825, and his own marriage to Maria Barber of Woodford in February 1826.

By now John had resumed his trade as a jobbing gardener and he cultivated his own half acre "with the skill of the professional and the dedication of an amateur". One report states that he worked for a time at Lawton's Pleasure Gardens, where a small collection of animals was kept as one of the attractions. (The gardens were located around a mill reservoir at Portwood; the site later became part of Stockport Gasworks.) No doubt the experience gained there encouraged John Jennison to think of the potential of his own plot, for in 1826, with the aid of his wife, he opened his garden on summer Sunday afternoons; the strawberries he produced were said to have been delicious. At this time there was no animal collection and the place became known as the Strawberry Gardens or, later, Jennison's Gardens.

Ir
st
wa
en
oc
ne
pla ... it and the young birds. The parent continued to feed its chicks through the netting and the novel sight drew crowds to the gardens. Jennison was quick to seize the opportunity created and added cages containing British birds, pheasants and macaws. The establishment was now open daily in summer, including Sundays and bank holidays, and an admission charge was made. Soon after, a brewhouse was built, together with a four horse stable, and the original house became a pub called the Adam & Eve. There was to be a difference between Jennison's enterprise and those of his competitors: his was a public house attached to a pleasure garden, not a public house with a pleasure garden.

Early Days at Belle Vue

By the mid-1830s the gardens, which by now included a sizeable collection of parrots, had attracted the attention of Manchester businessmen. One of these, George Gill of Heaton Norris, suggested to Jennison that he consider Belle Vue, on

An impression of John Jennison's Adswood property about 1835, viewed from the corner of Stockholm Road and Adswood Grove

the new road between Manchester and Hyde, as a more suitable outlet for his talents, and Jennison must have realised that his business could expand no more at Adswood. Maybe with this suggestion in mind, for which he would need capital, he took out a fresh mortgage in December 1835 for £300 and paid off an earlier mortgage of £80 taken out on the Adswood property in 1822. In June 1836 he took a lease of Belle Vue on six months' trial, keeping Adswood in full operation in the meantime. The trial period was evidently successful, as in December he took a 99 year lease on the property at a rent of £135 per annum, backdated to June.

Jennison offered the Strawberry Gardens at Adswood for sale or lease in the Stockport Advertiser on 3rd December, but it was not until 1838 that a Mr Bramwell took the premises on lease and placed a series of advertisements in the same newspaper:

"Bramwell's Zoological Gardens, late Jennison's, Adswood Lane, near Stockport. Mr J Bramwell returns thanks for encouragement since taking over the Gardens...he has added many rare and beautiful animals to his establishment ... wines, spirits, bottled and draught porter and ale, cider of the first quality and refreshments may be had. Admission to heads of families free."

Bramwell's advertisements ceased in mid-August 1838 and he was followed by another tenant whose lack of fortune was similar. Both had failed to appreciate the true spirit of the place and had turned it into a mere pub with gardens attached. The admittance of drinkers without payment had resulted in a change of emphasis which drove many of Jennison's old customers away.

In the early years of the century, lime (known locally as Ardwick Lime) had been dug from the land at Belle Vue. A system of waterways had been cut across the site to allow the lime to be carried to kilns in small boats. Although most of these had been filled in, a number of long narrow ponds remained, with the result that the ground was marshy in places and considered to be of poor agricultural quality.

The initial stimulus to the development of the area had been provided in 1818 when work on the turnpike road linking Manchester and Hyde (Hyde Road) began. In 1819, a lease was granted to one John Walker,

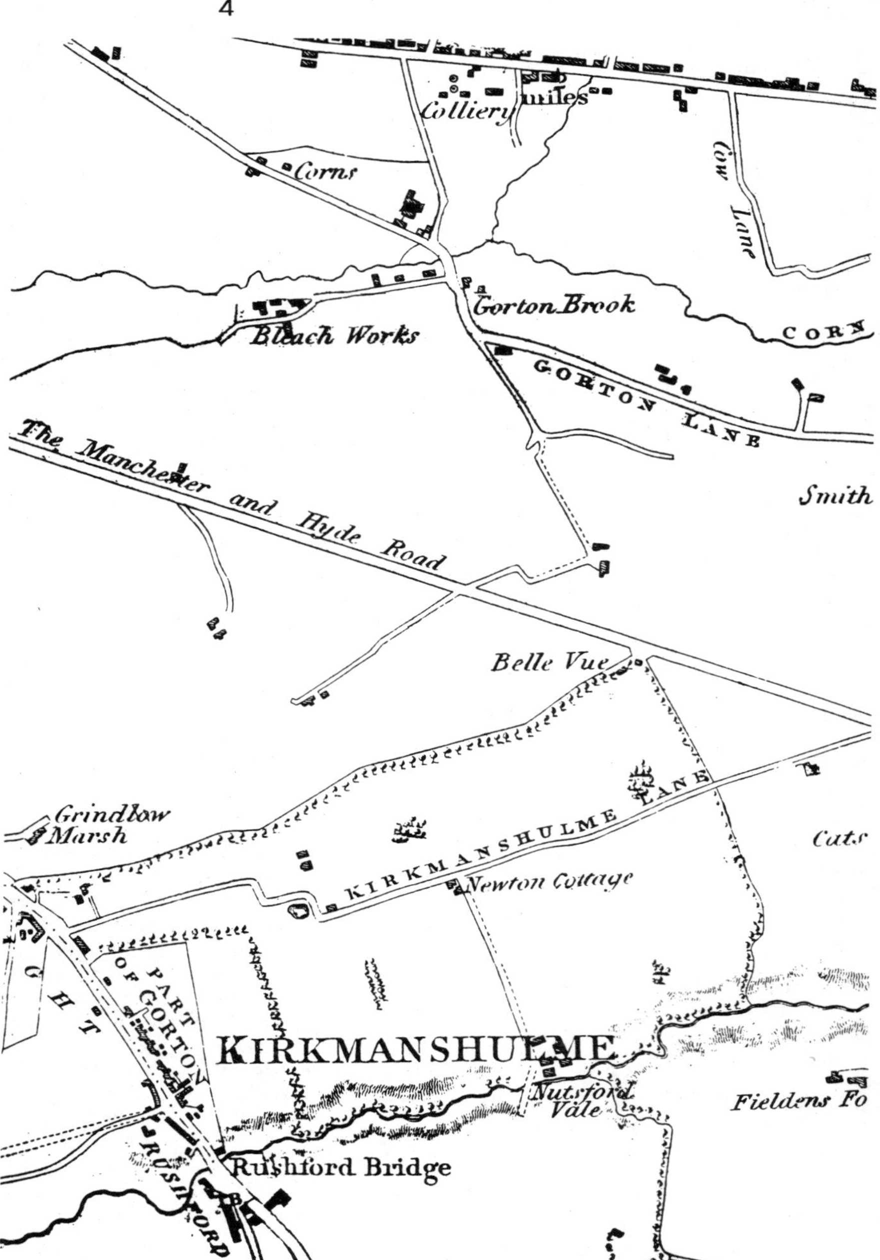

Hyde Road, Belle Vue House and neighbourhood in the 1820s. (From Johnson's plan of Manchester and District)

who built a public house called the Belle Vue House. The original building was half inn and half farmhouse, with its ground floor level some four feet above the roadway. On each side of the doorway, reached by steps, was a single room. On the left was the bar parlour, whilst the room on the right was used by the publican's family. The space beneath the ground floor comprised a public stable and a shippon. On the first floor was a verandah. Some 60 yards to the rear was a bowling green, planted round with shady trees, located in 2 acres of garden. Thirteen acres were pasture and the remaining 20 acres were given over to occasional uses such as racing or shooting.

In 1834 the lease was taken over by William Crisp who, it is said, introduced the sport of rabbit coursing on the 20-acre plot. This was the poor man's equivalent of hare coursing, then in vogue with the aristocracy of the area. Crisp also ran competitions on the bowling green, and advertised the establishment as the Belle Vue Tea Gardens.

John Jennison and his family left Adswood in February 1837. At Belle Vue he was in control of some $35\frac{1}{4}$ acres lying between Kirkmanshulme Lane and the then local government boundary between the townships of Ardwick and Kirkmanshulme. In December 1836 Jennison had felt confident enough to take, for an annual rent of £100, a tenancy of a further area that lay between his western boundary at Redgate Lane, then a mere footpath, and Stockport Road. Although the principal entrance to the gardens was then, as always, at Hyde Road, Jennison realised that the Gardens' potential would be increased if a second approach could be made from Stockport Road which, unlike Hyde Road, was toll free and of greater importance. Jennison soon found that he needed more capital than he had originally anticipated. He had been obliged to purchase a herd of Alderney cows from William Crisp and he had not been successful in selling Adswood. In 1838 he paid off his existing mortgage and took out a new one, provided by John Pownall, cheesefactor of Rostherne, and John Barratt, grocer of Altrincham, for the sum of £800 at an interest rate of 5% per annum.

The zoological collection was an early candidate for expansion. When the family moved from Adswood, it was said that all their possessions were carried on a single cart, with two or three cages hanging from the back, together with a woodcock belonging to Ann, Jennison's eldest daughter. The first advertisement, which appeared in the Manchester Guardian in May 1837, indicates the expansion of the collection:

"...The Public are respectfully informed, that the BELLE VUE GARDENS...are NOW OPEN to the public... (John Jennison) has collected a large number of very beautiful Birds, comprising parrots, parroquets, macaws, cockatoos, gold and silver pheasants, peacocks of different descriptions, swans, Canada geese, and various animals, which he intends placing in the grounds...During the Whitsun-week, a field of ten acres, belonging to the grounds, will be opened for the use of Sunday Schools, free of expense; and a band will be in attendance."

As to the identity of the "animals", we can only speculate. Rabbits, dogs, goats and a fox are strong possibilities, and even deer are suggested by some sources. Clearly, exotic species are not yet present as they would have merited a separate mention in the advertisement. Admission to the Gardens was 3d, returned in non-alcoholic refreshments, mostly milk and butter biscuits. At an early date, Jennison aroused the opposition of the wardens of St James's Church, Gorton, who ordered him to cease supplying customers during the times of Sunday services. His reputed reply was: "I am like thee, I make my living on Sundays". He was troubled no more by them.

Jennison had taken to his new property with vigour; the tasks facing him were many and the scale of the enterprise was completely different from Adswood. At an early date he built a cottage for his ageing mother: this was probably the one on Kirkmanshulme Lane at the northerly boundary of the property and known later as Belle Vue Cottage. He then enlarged the main house, forming a bigger bar and improving the outbuildings, which no doubt included the provision of a brewhouse so that he could brew his own beer, as at Adswood.

The zoological collection was initially housed in a shed, some 36 feet by 70 feet, to the right of the Hyde Road entrance. He continued to farm the 13 acres of pasture, but attended to the drainage of the race-ground at the Longsight end and replaced its hedge with a secure fence made of old barrel staves. Although the rabbit coursing events were considered to be the most valuable part of the business in 1836, and a financial necessity for Jennison, he showed no enthusiasm for the sport in view of the class of patron it tended to attract and left the organisation of the events to others. For the comfort of his better class visitors, he placed four arbours in the Gardens, which were still limited to the two acres adjacent to the main house and bowling green.

The Redgate Lane public footpath prevented Jennison from expanding the Gardens on to the additional area rented at the end of 1836 and leading up to Stockport Road, but in 1837 he did peg out the route of the great avenue linking the Hyde Road entrance with Stockport Road via the roads later known as Belle Vue Avenue and Newton Avenue.

The first two years proved to be a modest success, despite an early setback when Belle Vue House lost its carting customers. One day the regular carters turned up to find their usual stable crowded out with visitors to a rabbit coursing event. When Jennison refused to clear these out, the carters took their custom to the Plough at Gorton and were not to return.

In 1838 Jennison leased another 8 acres which formed the triangle between his property, Hyde Road and Kirkmanshulme Lane, where the Great Lake was dug in later years. At first, pits were dug to obtain clay for making the bricks used in the erection of various buildings in the Gardens. By May 1841 the area was being used as an extension to the Gardens; the pits were filled with water and advertised as an attraction:

"...Mr Jennison is happy to state that his collection of birds and beasts are in good and healthy condition and in addition to the pleasure

MANCHESTER ZOOLOGICAL GARDENS, HIGHER BROUGHTON.—The above extensive and picturesque GARDENS are NOW OPEN to the Public, and contain a Splendid Exhibition of rare and beautiful Animals and Birds, consisting of a Rhinoceros, Elephant, Lions, Tigers, Leopards, Hyænas, Puma, Wolves, Bears, Dromedary, Ostrich, Enues, &c. &c.
Admission, 1s.; children under 14 years of age, 6d.
Subscribers' tickets for the year ending the 30th April, 1839 (instead of the 25th March, as previously advertised), may be procured from the Secretary, 63, King-street, where rules and every further particulars may be obtained.

ZOOLOGICAL GARDENS.—Mrs. BAKEWELL, of Princess-street, respectfully announces to her Friends and the Public, that she has TAKEN the large and commodious REFECTORY at these Gardens, where visitors can be accommodated with tea, coffee, and other refreshments of the best quality, on reasonable terms.

VAUXHALL GARDENS, COLLYHURST.
JAMES POWNALL begs most respectfully to announce to his Friends and the Public, that he has taken and entered upon the above GARDENS; and that, on MONDAY, June 4th, he will give a GRAND GALA, on a scale of magnificence hitherto unequalled. The Fire Works will be of the most superb order ever seen in this part of the globe, by MADAME HENGLER, of the Jardin Turc, Paris, and Vauxhall Gardens, London. The Illumination will be on a most extensive scale.—Police officers will be in attendance.

Newspaper advertisements for Belle Vue's competitors at Higher Broughton and Collyhurst, June 1838 grounds of last year, there is now an extension of land which contains 6 beautiful fish ponds, stored with fish and it is presumed that the air blowing from these waters in warm weather must be most agreeable and pleasant to visitors who may resort here to enjoy the cooling shade."

Financial Difficulties and the Threat of Competition

Despite the encouraging signs, financial pressures had been building up. From May 1838 the chief rent on Adswood had not been paid and arrears of interest on the mortgage had accrued. The failure to sell Adswood or even to lease it to a secure tenant was a disadvantage. More important were the threats posed by the establishment of the Manchester Zoological Gardens at Higher Broughton and the building of the Manchester & Birmingham Railway.

The former had been initiated by a committee of aristocrats led by the Earl of Derby in 1836. Their aim was to create not a pleasure garden, but a zoological garden such as that at Regents Park, London, run for scientific and educational purposes. The gardens were laid out early in 1838 on a 15-acre site at the junction of what are now Bury New Road and Northumberland Street. The Zoological Gardens Company had some 1,800 shareholders, many from the aristocracy, who were lavish in their gifts of animals. The attractions included a lake 250 yards long, an archery ground, geological museum, bear pits, a maze and a lion house. The scope of the zoological collection exceeded that of Jennison's and for several years the Higher Broughton Zoological Gardens proved a serious competitor for Belle Vue. In its first six months of operation it made a profit of £2,100 and had some 42,000 visitors, many of whom were the better class of patron whom John Jennison was anxious to attract.

The other threat to Belle Vue, the building of the Manchester & Birmingham Railway, had also been initiated in 1836 and construction work started two years later. The railway sliced through the plot taken by Jennison at the end of 1836, and put paid to his idea of forming a separate approach from Stockport Road. As he held only a tenancy of this land, it is unlikely that he received compensation from the railway company. To add insult to injury, when the first stage of the new line, from Manchester to Stockport, was opened in June 1840, the station for Longsight was opened some distance from the gardens, at the point where the railway crossed Stockport Road.

Jennison realised that if he were to succeed on a grand scale, new initiatives were needed. He had to provide events and attractions to entice patrons in and encourage them to return, and also develop excursion traffic to bring in visitors from a far wider area. Other pleasure gardens had resorted to the provision of attractions for several years. There were firework displays at the Vauxhall Gardens and by 1841 even the Manchester Zoological Gardens Company, in a bid to keep up attendances, had succumbed to the holding of horticultural shows and firework displays.

Jennison's own attractions began in a modest way. On 12th April 1841 a footrace was held in which John Grimshaw of Gorton beat William Walker of Stockport. In the same year, a local landmark, the "Hollow Blasted Oak" of Yew Tree Farm, Gorton, was moved to the Gardens after a supposed existence of 500 years. On 2nd May 1842, "splendid fireworks" were exhibited by Signor Pietro (Mr Richardson) of Chapel House, Gorton, who had some years earlier undertaken the displays at the Vauxhall Gardens. On 4th September a Mr Moorhouse, the "flying tailor of Denton", prepared a kite, 20 feet tall, to carry him to a height of 200 feet. However, Mr Moorhouse had second thoughts on the wisdom of such a display and his kite ascended with only three 56lb weights attached.

The other innovation - the development of excursion traffic - was to take longer, although in 1840 there is said to have been an excursion from Macclesfield by canal which alighted at Gorton Bridge, about a mile from Belle Vue. Even if this had been undertaken with the swift "fly boats" of the day, it is difficult to see how it could have been a day excursion in view of the roundabout route and the numerous locks on the canals concerned.

It was the rapid expansion of the railway network which provided the necessary fillip that Jennison needed to develop excursion traffic. In May 1842 a small station was opened on the Manchester, Sheffield & Lincolnshire Railway at Gorton, some two miles from the Gardens. However, in the same month, the Manchester & Birmingham Railway relented and relocated the Longsight station adjacent to Kirkmanshulme Lane; three months later this line had opened in its entirety.

1842 - Year of Crisis

The year 1842 was a very testing time for Jennison. There was a general scarcity of money and a great deal of industrial unrest in the area. Even the rabbit coursing events at Belle Vue were prohibited for a time as the police would not permit crowds of such rough men to assemble. Matters were brought to a head when bankruptcy proceedings were in-

6¼ years rent to Mr Knight at £135 per annum	*£843 15s 0d*
Rent paid to Mr Lingard	*£150*
2½ years rent on 2 fields at £40 per annum	*£100*
6½ years wages, 3 female servants average £8 per annum each	*£156*
6½ years wages, 3 male servants average £13 per annum each	*£253 10s 0d*
6 years extra waiters, £20 per annum	*£120*
6½ years 2 men working in grounds at £52 per annum each	*£676*
6½ years keeping self, wife, 7 children, 6 servants at average of 4s per head per week each	*£1014*
6½ years clothing for self, wife, children, including doctors' bills and children's schooling at £100 per annum	*£650*
6½ years assessed and other taxes at £9.14s.4d each	*£63 3s 2d*
6½ years keeping birds and beasts at £200 per annum	*£1300*
Draining 20 acres of land at £7 per acre	*£140*
Enlarging house	*£50*
Building large cottage	*£100*
Building stained glass summer house	*£100*
Building aviary and fitting up with cages	*£150*
Building 7 brick summer houses	*£50*
Building yard, wall and convenience	*£40*
Building stand for racecourse	*£100*
Altering bar twice	*£40*
Fencing round 20 acres of ground	*£200*
6½ years tithes at £3.8s.3d per annum	*£22 3s 7½d*

The statement of John Jennison's expenditure at the time of his bankruptcy proceedings itiated against Jennison on 13th December by John Hadfield, a flour dealer, and William Drabble, a brewer, to whom Jennison owed £169-14s-4d and £237 respectively. On 26th December, Hadfield took over Adswood as trade assignee and James Stansfield Pott was the official assignee of the bankruptcy. Advertisements for the sale of Adswood appeared in 1843 and September 1844, although its value was insufficient to meet the arrears on the interest on the mortgage and the outstanding principal, which amounted to £1,100. No sale took place.

In the meantime, Jennison and his family were allowed to continue residing at Belle Vue and one of the petitioners' assistants, Peter Hatton, was dispatched there to collect cash owed. Jennison's assistant, Samuel Barber, denied that Jennison was at home, although afterwards, on affidavit, he stated that he had been told by Jennison to say that he was out. Subsequently three bailiffs were sent, but apparently behaved badly and one was later withdrawn. They were charged for beer and cigars consumed without authority.

The final examination of the bankruptcy proceedings took place on 21st January 1843. Fortunately, details of these are known and give a good impression of what had been achieved at Belle Vue since 1836.

Jennison's debts were approximately £1,340 and his total assets were £652-2s-5d, plus the value of the Gardens themselves. The creditors generously allowed him to keep a silver watch and £3-14s-6d in cash, but an attempt to sell the Gardens was fixed for 30th January. The purchaser had an option to buy "the animals, birds and cages and household effects at a valuation to be produced at the sale".

No sale took place, however, and a second date was set for 3rd March. This time the advertisement offered "twelve tons of hay, two horses, roller, bowls and a race stand". The auction was called off at the last minute when some of the creditors decided that their best chance for recovering their money was to wait for it to be earned by Jennison. One Stockport man is said to have accepted his dues in beer brewed by Jennison. The remaining creditors were paid off by a loan which Jennison somehow managed to obtain. He was obliged, however, to restrict his activities to his original site and give up the tenancies taken over in December 1836 and 1839.

The Gardens Continue in Business

John Jennison had managed to get through his difficulties by the skin of his teeth, but one of his major competitors, the Higher Broughton Zoological Gardens, had closed. Some accounts of Belle Vue state that John Jennison bought the contents of the Higher Broughton Zoo, but the records indicate to the contrary. Indeed, Jennison was hardly in a position to buy. What seems likely is that he was given some of the less exotic and smaller animals that could not be sold.

Jennison was quick to seize the opportunity created by the demise of the Manchester Zoological Gardens; this advertisement appeared in the Manchester Guardian in May 1843:

"...J JENNISON begs respectfully to return his grateful thanks to the Gentry and Public in general, for their liberal support for the last seven years, and to announce to them that the GARDENS are NOW OPEN, with a great variety of Foreign and British Animals and Birds...

All public Sunday schools will be admitted free during Whitsun week.

A quadrille band, conducted by the Cambrian family, so much esteemed at the Zoological Gardens, Higher Broughton, last year, will be in attendance every day during Whitsun week.

Parties can be accommodated by railway to the Longsight Station, for 3d., within 300 yards of the grounds.

An omnibus from the Bull's Head, London Road, during the race days, at half-past ten a.m. and at two, three, four, five, and six, p.m.; and from Belle Vue in the evening, at various times up to nine o'clock. On Sundays from the Bull's Head, every hour from four to nine, p.m. during the summer season, fares 6d. each."

On 17th July another footrace was held. The 1841 winner, John Grimshaw, raced Mr Wood of Levenshulme for £25. The former champion gave up after 25 yards and lost his £25. He afterwards disputed the validity of the race, resorted to litigation, lost, and as a result was imprisoned at Lancaster.

The 1843 season had been successful and it is reported that the creditors of the new loan were annoyed at being paid off so quickly. The following year, the Manchester & Birmingham Railway ran cheap trains to Longsight to bring visitors to the Gardens, which now had an entrance at Longsight. The 13 acres of pasture were incorporated into the Gardens and one of the ponds was enlarged to form the smaller, or Firework, lake of later years. A small building was erected on the central island to house a natural history museum and boats were placed on the lake.

The birds and animals, by now probably including monkeys, were said to be in excellent condition, as was the bowling green. A cricket ground had

TO BE

DISPOSED OF BY PRIVATE CONTRACT,

ALL that capital and newly-erected INN or PUBLIC-HOUSE, situate and being in Adswood, in the Parish of Cheadle, and county of Chester, together with the Brewhouse, Stabling, Gardens, and Appurtenances thereunto belonging, known by the name of or commonly called *Jennison's Gardens.*

The above property is freehold of inheritance, and the scite or ground plot thereof contains 2580 square yards; is situate about a mile and a half from the Stockport Market place, the same distance from Cheadle, and adjoining to the Manchester and Birmingham Railway. The house contains two most excellent entertaining rooms, and the Gardens are tastefully laid out with ornamental arbours for the purposes of refreshment; and a few years ago the premises were a place of great attraction, and would become so again in the hands of a spirited proprietor.

At a slight expence the premises might be converted into a desirable family residence.

For further particulars and to treat for the same, apply to Mr GEO. M. FERNS, SOLICITOR, Rostron Brow, Stockport.

1844 Stockport Advertiser notice about the sale of Adswood. It had been taken over by Jennison's creditors following his financial problems of two years before

been laid out and an individual named "Great Western" started a much-acclaimed walk in the Gardens on Easter Monday. His aim was to walk 1,000 miles in 1,000 hours, a feat which he easily achieved. The admission charge was 3d or 6d, the value of which was returned in refreshments, plus 1d for the band. The latter imposition was resented by visitors and it was soon dropped. The following year the charge was 6d, all returned in refreshments.

There was another, unsuccessful, attempt to sell Adswood in 1844. Three years earlier, before the financial troubles, members of John Jennison's family were living at Adswood and looking after the family interests there. The census of 1841 records his son and daughter, John (aged 14) and Elizabeth (aged 12) at the Adam and Eve with their grandmother, Elizabeth Jennison (aged 80). John junior was listed as "publican".

Accounts of the family's involvement with Adswood are sometimes contradictory. George Jennison, John's grandson, writing in the 1920s, states that John leased the property from his assignees in 1845 and installed his son as manager, when some of the Belle Vue collection was spared to fill the old cages. George also says that monkeys were included in the Adswood collection for the first time at this date, leading to the property's nickname, the "Monkey House". However, a contributor to the Stockport Advertiser, writing in 1885, remembered that in 1835 John Jennison's collection included "a large cage occupied by a few monkeys" and that "the monkeys became more numerous and of more varied tribes".

Whatever the circumstances surrounding the younger Jennison's stay at Adswood, the move to re-establish the family business there was not a success. George comments that John junior was "bold in undertaking work", but he was "slack in carrying it out" and he lacked his father's skills as a botanist or naturalist.

Belle Vue's novelties for 1845 included equestrians, rope dancing and performing dogs. In 1846, a "dissolving diorama" appeared, and a fireworks display by Messrs Francklin & Carroll of the Royal Vauxhall Gardens, London. There was a visit by Cooke's Circus and on 21st and 28th June a "complimentary levee" was held. The Manchester Brass Band was engaged in Whit week. Mr Moorhouse of Denton made another attempt to ascend in a skip attached to a kite. Again his nerve failed him and he sent up his collection of weights instead.

In May, a competitor opened the Pomona Gardens on the south-west side of Manchester, but this did not adversely affect Belle Vue, nor did it possess a zoological collection.

A Visit to Belle Vue in 1847

1847 saw more progress and this year the first guide book was produced. It cost 4d and was printed by John Bradshaw of Church Street, Manchester. The contents were drawn up by Robert Dibb, sometimes referred to as the "Wharfedale Poet". The guide contains a lithograph engraving showing a bird's eye view of the Gardens and the racecourse. Most of the zoological collection consisted of birds of South American origin, but other animals are mentioned - silver fox, Australian dingo, raccoons, Brahmin bull, red and fallow deer, Cape, Egyptian and Australian sheep, Armenian monkeys, lesser white rhesus monkeys, American squirrels, wild cats, mongoose, white cat, red and blue coati mundi, hedgehog, guinea pigs, rabbits, armadillos, common hare and a bear.

The following passages from the guide convey the atmosphere of a visit to the Gardens in 1847:

"The Visitor on entering the Gardens from the Hyde Road, after passing the 'Entrance Gate', and turning immediately to the right must first observe the Magnificent Weeping Ash... under which is an extensive Arbour amply accommodated with neatly painted tables and seats."

The original aviary, built by Jennison ten years earlier, was still in use, containing other animals as well as birds, but there was also a "Spacious Peacock's Cage", a "Yew Tree Aviary", "Stands for Maccaws and Cockatoos" and a "Large Aviary with Glass Dome". Continuing on our tour, we find a *"Large Painted Glass Arbour, the interior of which is lighted with splendidly Stained Glass Windows; whilst Allegorical Paintings beautify the walls.*

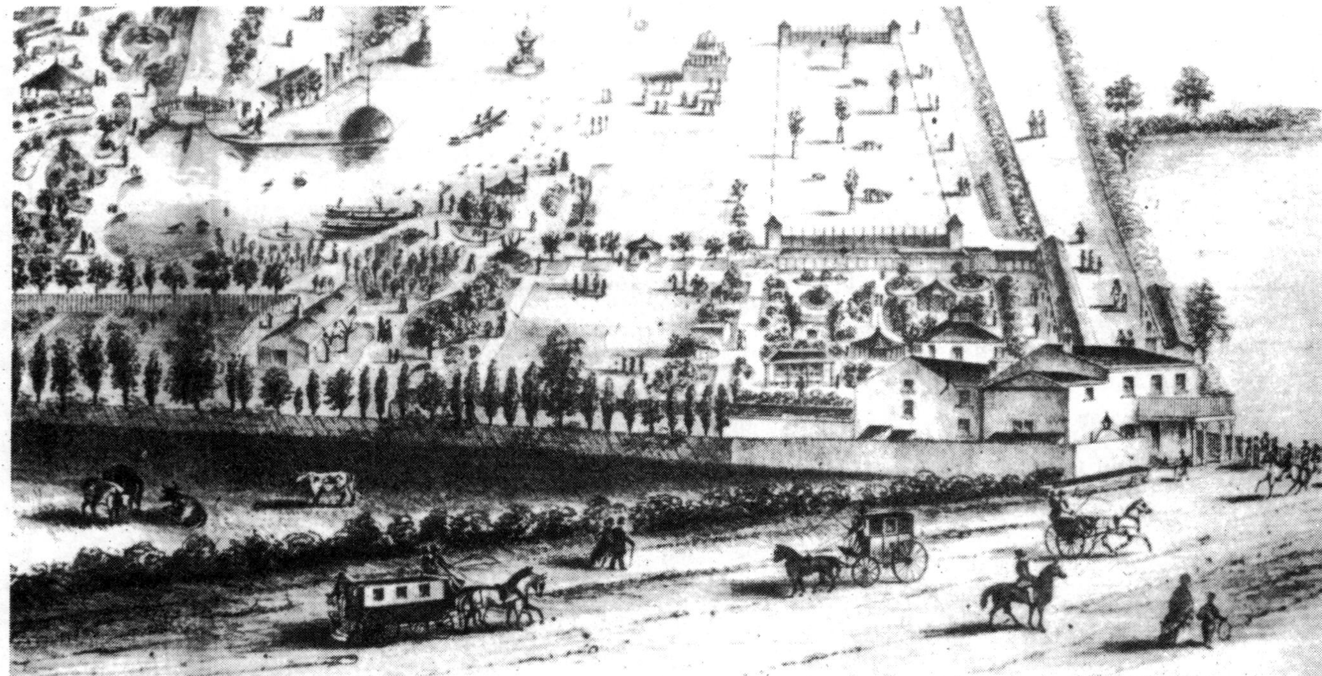

Hyde Road, the Belle Vue Inn and part of the Gardens from a lithographic print which appeared in the first guide book, published in 1847

On our left are 16 Spacious Arbours, with slate roofing, thoroughly impervious to the rain and beautifully secluded by shrubs, trees, and flowers; whilst near the Bar for Refreshments is a Tomb Stone to the memory of a faithful Dog...

The Bowling Green...is bounded on the left by Five Neat & convenient Ornamental Arbours, roofed and divided into compartments, and surmounted by gilded representations of Birds, Beasts and Reptiles; whilst to our extreme right is an immense Area studded with Trees, Shrubs, Flowers, Lakes, Fountains and Grottos...One side of the Green is set apart for Dancing, and the Lovers of this delightful exercise may enjoy themselves to the fullest extent.

During the Summer Months, THE BELLE VUE QUADRILLE BAND is here placed from Two o'clock in the Afternoon until Dusk..."

A variety of swans, geese and other birds were present on the lake, whilst *"To our right is a Bower in the Chinese Style, with Weeping Elm in centre, whilst to our left are innumerable clumps of the most varied and splendid Shrubs and Flowers; round the Lake are a quantity of Rustic Chairs...*

Passing by the Pond for Geese, &c. we arrive at the Entrance of the Cave...Having passed through the Cave we suddenly find ourselves in a 'little Fairy Dell' or Secluded Retreat, in the centre of which is a Bear on the top of a Pole, and here the lovers of 'Pic-Nic Parties' may enjoy themselves...

Passing along the Serpentine Walks...we arrive at The Rustic Arbour, formed of Nine Grotesque Trees, the centre one of which is the Ruins of the Celebrated Gorton Oak, which was struck by Lightning and the rents of which are visible: at the foot of each Tree are spacious chairs. Still bearing to the left we see the RUSTIC BRIDGE, with the following inscription in wood letters. TO THE MUSEUM.

...We are now on THE ISLAND... In the centre on a large Rockery is the Carved Figure of Flora the Goddess of Flowers. At each end, on Rockeries, are Two Monkeys elevated on Pedestals, a shell arbour with King William the Fourth seated, surrounded by several Carved Figures, Van Amburg taming the Lion, Elephant with superb Castle and Attendant, a Lion reposing, likewise The Turret and Clock, added to which there is a Cavern which extends from one end of the Island to the other.

On returning from THE MUSEUM, we come to the Small Lake for Gold & Silver Fish, with Two small ornamental Bridges and Clump in the centre of the Island, to our left is another great object of interest, viz. A Large Shell Terrace Flower Bed, with circular and likewise diamond Fixings, formed entirely of Shells; in the centre is a Weeping Willow and a variety of Fuschias, Petunias, Mimulas, Calceolarius, &c, whilst the basement comprises a selection of choice Verbenas...

The Maze or Labyrinth, modelled from the one at Hampton Court... In the centre of the Maze are Two Octagonal Gothic Aviaries, with Glass Domes, Green Slated Roofs and pendant Wood Scrolls, the whole supported by Marbled Pilasters. One is lighted with magnificently Stained Glass Windows, the intermediate space being filled by Reflecting Mirrors, which gives the appearance of an innumerable quantity of richly plumaged Birds. The other is embellished with a Superb Specimen of Chinese Needlework, wrought on Scarlet Cloth, with Gold, &c, in the most elegant devices; the most prominent of which are the Lyre Bird, Dolphins, and Birds of Paradise, the above production is singularly beautiful, and is allowed by all Ladies who have seen it to be the most elaborate specimen ever imported from the Celestial Empire. On leaving the Maze and passing the Gothic Cottage, we proceed on our left by the banks of the Lake, when our attention is directed to The Large Dolphin Fountain, which by the aid of a powerful Steam Engine erected in the building opposite to us is throwing up the water 30 feet high..."

THE HAND BOOK

TO THE

ZOOLOGICAL GARDENS,

BELLE VUE,

HYDE ROAD, NEAR MANCHESTER,

CONTAINING A FULL

LIST OF THE BIRDS & ANIMALS,

WITH

DESCRIPTIVE NOTICES OF THEIR HABITS, &c. &c.

ALSO A

CATALOGUE

OF THE

MUSEUM OF NATURAL HISTORY, CURIOSITIES, &c.

PROPRIETOR, Mr. JENNISON.

MANCHESTER:
PRINTED BY JOHN BRADSHAW, 6, CHURCH STREET.
1847.

Title page of the first Belle Vue guide book

One particular attraction described in the guide is the "Monster Globe Stand": *"A square wooden building with two flights of stairs, and surmounted by two tiers of Ornamental Balustrades; on the top is a Terrestrial Globe, 20 Feet in Circumference, which is made of Zinc, and has attracted considerable notice from its novelty and bulk..."*

A deer paddock, 144ft by 75ft, is mentioned, also a new 35ft-high grandstand, capable of holding 4,000 people. The original grandstand, erected in the late 1830s, is described as having accommodation for 1,500 persons. The Gardens were described as being suitable for the holding of promenade concerts and balls, floral and horticultural shows, meetings of scholars and "convivial anniversaries of benefit societies". They were also open in the winter, with ice skating on the lake.

Successes and Failures 1847-51

The first recorded excursion train to Belle Vue brought a party from Lord Street Sunday School, Macclesfield, on 22nd June 1847. This was an isolated event, as neither Jennison nor the railway companies were yet willing to guarantee the 300 or so passengers needed to justify the running of such trains. This reluctance was not to last for long.

POMONA GARDENS, HULME, MANCHESTER.—On Monday next, the **FOURTH** Magnificent **REPRESENTATION** of the **STORMING OF AMOY**, in China, will take place.

The Manchester Borough Brass Band, and an excellent Quadrille Band, will be in attendance. In the Evening the Gardens will be brilliantly Illuminated.

Admission, 1s. each.—Steamers on the Irwell, from Victoria Bridge, Albert Bridge, and the Hare and Hounds, Water-street; and Omnibuses, from Market-street, to the Gardens, every half-hour.

More competition - a newspaper advertisement from July 1851

One of Jennison's unsuccessful innovations of 1847 was his attempt to turn the 20-acre raceground into a proper racecourse. The course was three-quarters of a mile long, running around the raceground, with a quarter-mile straight section through the centre for sprinters. The idea for such a racecourse followed the closure of the nearby Gorton Racecourse at Gorton Hall.

A race meeting was held on 29th May 1847, the prize being the Tradesman's Cup, worth 15 sovereigns. A trotting sweepstake had prizes of 3 sovereigns and a pony race a prize of 1 sovereign. A second race was held on 13th August, in which 27 horses were entered, and there was another trotting race the following day.

The racecourse was not a success because of competition from elsewhere. The Gorton Racecourse soon reopened and 1847 saw the opening of the New Manchester Racecourse at Castle Irwell. Racing was held at Belle Vue on a smaller scale in 1848; on 27th May Mr Whitehead's pony was matched to gallop two miles in six minutes for £30, and in September the "annual" Belle Vue Races were held. They were not repeated, although the sprint running track remained in use for a few years.

May 1848 saw the Manchester Open Tulip Show and a "grand floral and horticultural show". The following year Jennison felt sufficiently confident to purchase a leasehold interest in 4.1 acres between the Redgate Lane entrance and Longsight Station, part of the land he had been obliged to give up in 1842/3. The lithographic print in the 1847 guide shows this area laid out with tree-lined avenues leading to the Longsight entrance, but this was probably a representation of what Jennison had in mind for the future. In the same year, a grand supper was held at Belle Vue for the workmen who had recently completed the new City Gaol (or Belle Vue Gaol) on the eastern side of Hunters Lane.

ZOOLOGICAL GARDENS,
BELLEVUE, HYDE ROAD,
MANCHESTER.

Mr. JENNISON, PROPRIETOR,

Trusts that the Importance of this Place of Public Resort, equal in reference to the Capital expended in bringing the GARDENS to their present State of Perfection—the Novel and Attractive Style in which they are disposed—their Unparalled Extent—the Vast Assemblage of Objects of Interest, Natural and Artificial which they present—the Facility and Cheapness of Access—the Succession of Public Entertainments, introduced during the Season, and his determination to maintain the Strictest Decorum and Propriety in their Management, may induce many to avail themselves of a means of Recreation, so Cheap, Healthful and Improving, and confirm the resolution still further to render BELLEVUE Worthy the Support of the Community of Manchester and the Neighbourhood by

The Frequent Introduction of Additional Features of Attraction.

Since Last Season, the Improvements and Additions have been on an Extensive and Varied Scale, amongst these may be named the Erection of a

SPACIOUS BUILDING

FOR THE BETTER CONVENIENCE OF THE

MUSEUM OF CURIOSITIES,

STUFFED ANIMALS AND BIRDS,

And other Objects, to which *Great Additions* have recently been made, including Two Very Fine Specimens of the

LION AND LIONESS.

A NEW MONKEY HOUSE,

Has also been Constructed, in which is placed a* Monster Cage, *21 Feet in Height and Covering an Area of upwards of 600 Square Feet.

A GYMNASIUM,

Complete in every detail, has been introduced for the Healthful Recreation of frequenters to the Gardens. To the previous Extensive Zoological Collection may be mentioned,

The Addition of Remarkably Fine Specimens of the Leopard, Striped Hyæna, Ocelot or Tiger Cat, Wolf, Bear, Zebu Bull, Ostrich, Vulture, and innumerable other varieties.

In the Grounds the Numerous Serpentine and other Ornamental Walks and Promenades have been entirely renovated and a Large Variety of Exotic and other Plants added.

THE EXTENSIVE SHEET OF WATER,

On which Float many Small Pleasure Boats for the further Accommodation of the Public, continues to be a source of Great Attraction ; and the

ELIZABETHAN MAZE,

Affords much Amusement, especially to Juveniles.

To the Admirers of Horticultural and Decorative Gardening, the Hot Houses and Green Houses, Ornamental Parterres, Fountains, Shaded Walks, Rockeries, Grottoes, Caves, Arbours, &c., present a Pleasing Assemblage of Objects for contemplation. The

SPACIOUS DANCING PLATFORM,

Has been enlarged to an Area of upwards of 15,000 Square Feet, and in the event of Unfavourable Weather, Accommodation is provided in the Gardens for the shelter of thousands.

Three Floral and Horticultural Shows are held Annually in the Gardens, at stated intervals.

BELLEVUE is Situated Two Miles from Manchester, on the Road to Hyde; it also adjoins the London and North-Western Line, at the Newly-Erected Longsight Station, which renders it easy of approach from Manchester, Stockport, Macclesfield, and the Stations on the Line to Crewe; it is also within Half a Mile of the Gorton Station on the Sheffield and Lincolnshire Line.

Visiters can be Accommodated with Wines and Spirits of the Finest Qualities, Guiness's Bottled Stout, Breakfasts, Dinners, Tea and other Refreshments, at a Moderate Charge.

A Powerful Brass Band in daily attendance during the Summer Season.

N. B.—The Gardens are open every day throughout the year, as in Winter they are very appropriate for SKATING, the Waters being very extensive and less than three feet in depth, which renders this amusement perfectly Safe.

1850 advertisement, drawing the public's attention to the new Natural History Museum and new accommodation for the monkeys

1850 saw the final parting of Jennison with Adswood when he sold his "equity of redemption" for £5, although in reality control of the property was vested in the assignees under the mortgage. It became a private dwelling known as Adswood House.

The original raceground grandstand was used for the Great Northern Tulip Show in 1850. Messrs Brierley and Griffiths were engaged to put on a Lilliputian Circus, including a whole range of "faery steeds, juvenile equestrians, tightrope dancers and clowns". Extra boats were placed on the lake and a gymnasium was provided for children. During Whit Week "three efficient brass bands" were advertised "in order that dancing may continue during the entire day without interruption". The floral and horticultural show was repeated and on 27th August M Jullien and "his unrivalled band" and the "splendid band of the 3rd Dragoon Guards", conducted by Mr Rungeling, appeared. Special trains ran to Longsight Station every fifteen minutes and the admission was 2/-, the proceeds being split equally between Jullien and Jennison. At the end, the two bands played the National Anthem, each bar punctuated by the discharge of a cannon. Also that year, a Mr Atkins of Liverpool put on a firework display which included colossal transparencies of the

Duke of Wellington and Prince Albert on horseback, surrounded by streams of fire.

In September, Herr Kjellberg appeared:

"Kjellberg, the celebrated water king ... will introduce his military exercises in the national costume of Sweden whilst accomplishing the unparalleled task of walking on the water. He will also undertake the novel and daring act whilst on the water of drawing a boat filled with persons. The mechanical invention by which these feats are accomplished has occupied the attentions of Herr Kjellberg during many years; his patience and industry in bringing it to perfection have at length been rewarded with success."

In 1850 the Natural History Museum was removed from the island to the upper floor of a new building near the Hyde Road entrance. Its exterior was adorned by a painting by J F Makin entitled, "Adam and Eve in Paradise". The old museum building was used to display a model of Hobart Town, Tasmania. The ground floor of the new building housed an aviary and stabling, although at the Hyde Road end a 600 cubic feet "monster Monkey Cage" was provided and a nearby square cage was used for the display of cockatoos.

The Tulip Show was repeated in 1851 and Mr Wells, a ventriloquist, appeared in the old museum building. The imposing Longsight entrance was built at a cost of £1,000, in the same style as the nearby City Gaol. A spacious room above the central archway was capable of holding 500 people. Similar alterations were made at the Hyde Road entrance.

Apart from the stonemasonry, undertaken by a Mr William Dowgill, all the work was done by Jennison's own labour force, a practice he adopted at an early date. A spacious refreshment bar was built, also an "octagonal orchestra" or bandstand. A company of equestrians and clowns with a stud of horses and miniature ponies was on display every afternoon, and firework displays were put on by a Mr Merriday. The National Independent Order of Oddfellows held their grand fete, the procession from Salford Town Hall being led by the Manchester Borough Brass Band. In the evenings, another "efficient brass band", under the direction of Mr Hough, performed "a selection of the most popular Quadrilles, Polkas, Waltzes and Schottisches". By now, the old bowling green had been removed in order to make way for a wooden dancing platform on the northern side of the firework lake. The aviary in the ground floor of the new museum building was replaced by a den for "wild beasts", the first inhabitants being leopards, which bred that year. Yaks, porcupines and kangaroos were also acquired in 1851 from the dispersal of the private menagerie of the Earl of Derby. Two jaguars were added in 1852.

The improvements continued throughout 1852. The lake was increased in size, made more uniform in shape and provided with a new landing stage. The museum and the wild beast dens beneath were extended. The outdoor dancing platform was relaid. A gasworks was built to the right of the Hyde Road entrance, at some distance along the boundary of the gardens, by a Mr Mason of Ardwick. John Jennison is said to have believed that Manchester Corporation would never extend its own gas supplies out to Belle Vue. At first, two gas holders were provided, then a larger one, the total capacity of the works being 13,000 cubic feet. The 1852 attractions included an "Eccolobium", or egg-hatching machine, and the ruins of a building employed in testing Mr Phillips' Patent Fire Annihilator could be seen, together with the apparatus itself. Also displayed was a model of a First Class Man o' War, constructed for the 1851 Great Exhibition at Crystal Palace.

After overcoming the threat of closure brought about by his near bankruptcy in 1842, John Jennison had established the Gardens on a firm financial footing and the business expanded as a result. However, the year 1851 marked a significant watershed in the development of Belle Vue, for then the pace of expansion noticeably increased. The stimulus for this new phase in the Gardens' history arose out of Jennison's visit to the Great Exhibition.

The wooden dancing platform and Firework Lake, from a drawing which appeared in Belle Vue guide books of the 1890s

JOHN JENNISON'S YEARS OF SUCCESS 1852-69

Firework Displays, Balloon Ascents and Other Attractions

The increased vigour that John Jennison was applying to the development of the Gardens was evidenced by regular newspaper advertisements. But the main change from 1852 onwards was the transformation of the firework displays. On his visit to London, Jennison had seen the displays at the Surrey Zoological Gardens and was so impressed by these that he engaged Mr George Danson, the scenic artist of the Surrey Gardens and the London Colosseum, to come to Manchester with his two sons to organise the Belle Vue displays.

The Dansons painted a large-scale scenic background, known as the Picture and covering some 30,000 square feet of canvas, and men were employed to act out a scenario of some major historical event, usually incorporating a battle. The first show, "The Bombardment of Algiers" on 22nd May, was an immediate success, being seen by 1,800 people. However, in comparison with the shows of later years, it was a modest affair, employing only some 25 men and utilising 300 rockets, 25 large shells and 50 Roman candles, provided by Mr Bruce of London and Dublin. The total cost for the season was slightly over £1,100, of which Danson received £400. The display was located on the island where the museum had been. This was an ideal position, the water of the lake mirroring and multiplying the light, keeping the spectators out of danger and obliging them to see the display from its proper perspective. In addition, the space behind the island could be closed off easily.

To accommodate spectators, an elevated gallery, 180ft by 24ft, was erected, capable of seating 4,000 and allowing shelter underneath. Admission to the Gardens on firework days was 6d before 4pm, 1/- thereafter. Special trains ran to Longsight every half hour until 10pm. In October, Jennison introduced his own omnibus service along Hyde Road, running between the city and the Plough at Gorton.

The successful events of 1852 were marred by a tragedy on 2nd June. At 7pm Giuseppe Lunardini, "the celebrated Spanish aeronaut", was to make a balloon ascent with Jennison's eldest son, John. (Senor Lunardini was, in fact, a London oilcloth maker called James Goulston.) The 40ft high balloon had been partially inflated with gas produced at Belle Vue the previous day and on the day of the ascent it was filled to 19,000 cubic feet, 4,000 cubic feet short of its capacity because rainy conditions made the material somewhat water-logged. The deficiency was not considered serious. The rain delayed the start for half an hour, then a slight lull allowed the ascent to take place, although with only Goulston on board. The balloon rose into a cloud, the rain started again and it was next seen at Lees, near Oldham. The tragedy occurred at Stone Breaks, near Springhead. Evidently Goulston had difficulty in releasing gas from the balloon in order to descend, and let out a grappling iron. This engaged the ground, but the resulting jerk threw him out of the basket and he caught his leg on its netting. Hanging by the leg, he was killed by being dashed against a stone wall and being dragged for 280 yards before the balloon came to rest and rescuers were able to get to him.

At the inquest, it was stated that Goulston had made 50 previous ascents, although this had been his first solo trip, and that the gas could easily have been released with the aid of a passenger. It was alleged that Jennison had insisted on Goulston ascending, despite the poor weather, but more witnesses spoke to the contrary and the wording of Jennison's advertisement (that the ascent was dependent on the right weather conditions) weighed favourably in the mind of the coroner.

Improvements for 1853 included the extension of the lakeside terrace, the building of a bakery next to the gasworks (and sharing its chimney), the building of new greenhouses at the northern end of the Kirkmanshulme Lane boundary in what was then the kitchen garden, and the laying out of Belle Vue Avenue and The Avenue (now known as Olwen Avenue), both tree lined, linking the Longsight entrance with Longsight Station and Kirkmanshulme Lane respectively. It was intended to build "desirable residences" bordering these roads, but only three were built at a later date on Belle Vue Avenue. Called Belle Vue Place, the properties were named Bamford House, Dunscar House and Stanholme House and accommodated members of the next generation of the Jennison family.

The London & North Western Railway laid an additional siding at Longsight Station, capable of handling trains of 50 carriages. Within the Gardens, the tree-lined avenue was continued towards the Hyde Road entrance, along the line pegged out by Jennison in 1837. Some aviaries had to be moved in the process. Work was started on five statues, the first being of the Duke of Wellington. Part of the race-

George Danson, Belle Vue's first scenic artist

ground was given a lofty brick wall to form a 2-acre paddock. At the Longsight end of this paddock, a range of brick buildings was erected. The first of these contained a swimming bath, 180ft long, 60ft wide and 3ft to 5ft deep. It was located on the site of one of the old ponds and was surrounded by dressing rooms where towels were provided. Next to this, a range of cages was built, with a central corridor, for housing deer, gazelles, llamas, alpacas, kangaroos and zebu. At one end was an aviary. The range of cages formed the nucleus of what came to be known as the Paddock House.

A bear pit with stone-sided walls, sleeping dens and a central raised platform for three Russian brown bears, previously kept in cages beneath the museum, was provided on the north-eastern side of the lake, and a cage for "Asiatic bears" followed shortly afterwards. Other animals acquired included a pelican, an African lioness, two genets, an African ostrich, three drill baboons and a pair of Chinese lovebirds.

Attractions for 1853 included Signor Gomez the Archer and Miss MacDonald, the celebrated giantess, who paraded in Highland costume. A hawking exhibition was arranged for 6th April with Mr Barns, the "celebrated Scottish falconer". This was postponed until 13th and 14th April because of bad weather. The fireworks were on a more lavish scale, seventy men and boys being employed, and the cost was £1,500. The displays were extremely popular, so much so that crowds climbed on to the roofs of the refreshment rooms and the bandstand, causing part of the former to collapse.

A three-roomed firework shop was erected at the Longsight entrance and a small lake, 50ft long, was created at the northern end of the new paddock to house the waterfowl and other birds which could no longer be kept in safety on the main lake, now known as the Firework Lake or Picture Lake. Beneath the spectators' stand, erected the previous year, was a large painting and work room, used over the winter for the painting of the Picture and also capable of functioning as a refreshment room, with large sliding doors at its front. Attached to this was a small modelling room, used to display a miniature of the Picture, made by the Dansons as an aid to the construction of the full-scale set.

Musical Contests

The most important innovation for 1853 was the annual Brass Band Contest. Belle Vue had possessed its own brass band for a number of years, but Jennison's visit to the Great Exhibition made him revise his opinion about the value of such music in the Gardens. In brass band circles, there is still controversy as to who originated the idea for the competitions at Belle Vue. Years later, Enderby Jackson claimed the credit, in particular for drawing up the list of bands to be invited. He had earlier organised a series of contests at Hull and later arranged a series at the Crystal Palace. The commonly accepted version is that Jennison was encouraged to consider the contests by James Melling, the conductor of the City Royal Brass Band, then appearing at the Pomona Gardens.

As a trial, a drum and fife competition was organised for 1852. The weather was good and the crowds were described as "extrovert, but well behaved". Heartened by this, Jennison announced that the contest would be repeated in 1853 and that "he would further organise an advanced tested system of educating higher culture in the loftier spheres of musical art among the working classes of Lancashire and Yorkshire through the medium of carefully organised competitions for amateur brass bands".

Some weeks before the contest in September (picked to coincide with Gorton Wakes Week) Jennison invited leaders of brass bands in Lancashire, Cheshire and Yorkshire to compete for a series of prizes. Entry was £1, professional players were not allowed, each band was required to consist of at least ten performers and each band made its own choice of two pieces. Jennison contributed £20 for the first prize, to which was added the entrance money; subsequent prizes were £16, £6, £4 and £2. Eight bands entered, with a total of 100 performers. On the day the weather was favourable and an audience of 16,000 turned up. The supplies of food were exhausted half way through the proceedings.

The contest took place in the open and was due to start at 10.00am, but the delay of a special train from Leeds meant that it did not start until after 2pm. Even then the Mossley Band had still not arrived, and were obliged to play later. The pieces included the "Hallelujah Chorus", the overture to "Tancredi" and Haydn's "The Heavens are Telling", played by the Bramley Temperance and Mossley Temperance Sax Horn Bands. The judges, who were

George Danson's painting of Hyde Road from the entrance to Belle Vue. On the right is the lane which became Belle Vue Street. The painting was given to the City Art Gallery in 1947

carefully screened from the bands, were Mr Oakden, bandmaster to the 1st Royal Dragoons; Mr Ellwood, bandmaster to the Earl of Ellesmere, and Mr Dowlingate, late bandmaster to the 21st Regiment.

First prize was won by the Mossley Band, followed by the Dewsbury, Bramley Temperance and Bury Bands.

The 1853 contest virtually established the brass band and the brass band contest as they are today. The winners, the ten-strong Mossley Band, demonstrated the effectiveness of valved instruments and keyed bugles, ophicleides, etc, which until then had featured in bands, quickly disappeared. The success of the contests also demonstrated the popularity of the brass band over the wind and reed bands, which hitherto had been as common as brass bands.

In the wider context of the Gardens' development, the contests established Belle Vue as a popular place for railway excursions. Some £700 was received from the railway companies for excursion admissions in 1853, and a similar amount in 1854. Around £2,000 was received for 67,000 admissions in 1855. Excursion trains were run to coincide with other events, particularly Jullien's concerts, held annually in August. Access to the Gardens was considerably improved in July 1855 when a small station was opened on the Manchester, Sheffield & Lincolnshire line at Pottery Lane, a continuation of Belle Vue Street. This was a more convenient stopping place

John Ellwood, one of the adjudicators at the first Brass Band Contest in 1853

BRASS BAND CONTEST, Monday, 4th September, at the ZOOLOGICAL GARDENS, BELLE VUE, Manchester. **First prize, £20; second, £10; third, £6; fourth, £4;** fifth, £3; **and sixth, £1.—The following bands have entered for competition:—**

Name of Band.	No. of performers.	Name of leader.
Mossley Brass Band	14	William Seel.
Foxhill Bank, near Accrington	16	Hy. Hargreave
Batley, near Leeds	16	David Colbeck.
Bury	14	James Binns.
Milburn, Leeds	17	Herbert Milburn.
Barnsley	13	George Wray
Shelly, near Huddersfield	11	Geo. Earnshaw.
Whitworth, near Rochdale	10	Joseph Law.
Heckmondwike, near Leeds	12	George Brook
Accrington	13	Thomas Bradley.
Railway Foundry, Leeds	16	Richard Smith.
Mossley Temperance Sax-horn	10	William Taylor.
Dewsbury, near Leeds	16	John Peel.
Victoria, Batley, near Leeds	13	John Farrar.

The successful band, in addition to the first prize, will also receive a contré bass, or bombardon, with all the recent improvements, and German silver mountings, value £10. 10s. presented by Mr. Joseph Higham, Victoria Bridge, Manchester, The National Anthem, "God save the Queen," to be played by the whole of the performers at once. This will be performed at the close of the contest, and before the judges' decision is announced.

The BURNING OF MOSCOW will be represented, after the contest, with new and brilliant effects.—Admission, as on ordinary gala days, 6d. each before four o'clock; after that hour, 1s. each.

Advertisement for the 1854 Brass Band Contest

for excursion trains than the station at Gorton.

The new station, first called "Pottery Lane", was renamed "Ashbury's for Openshaw" in November 1855, after the adjoining wagon-builders who had paid for its erection. In August 1856 it was renamed again, "Ashbury's for Belle Vue".

The 1854 contest attracted 14 bands and 20,000 visitors. In addition to the cash prize, the winning band was presented with a "bombardon", given by a Mr Higham, a Manchester music dealer. Earlier, in June, a reed band contest attracted an audience of 8,000. The first prize was £16 and a cocoawood clarinet, also presented by Mr Higham.

Further Developments

Improvements carried out in 1854 included the enlargement of the bandstand, now called the Arabesque Orchestra, between the dancing platform and the original garden attached to Belle Vue House, still used for seating arbours. The bandstand could rotate to face either direction and its roof, 40 feet high, was decorated with coloured statues of Canova's Dancing Girls. The statuary in the Gardens was now complete: Nelson and Apollo Belvedere stood next to Wellington and elsewhere were smaller statues of Diana, Mercury, Venus, Hygeia, Hebe, Hercules, Children with Nests, Boy with Thorn, Solitude, Cromwell and Joan of Arc.

Two stone lions adorned the Longsight entrance, the avenue inside the grounds was paved at a cost of £1,000 and the whole Gardens was surrounded by a wall, 11ft high. A 30ft length of this was blown down by high winds early in the year. The dancing platform had been extended again and more boats were put on the lake, including a paddle steamer, the Little Britain, bought by Jennison's son, Charles, at Liverpool. It is said that the boat had been a government order, built for shallow river work in India. Belle Vue's own omnibus was making trips to Manchester by both Hyde Road and Stockport Road, and took passengers from the foot of the firework stand immediately after the displays. The bus service was not a success, however, and it was discontinued after 1855.

The Natural History Museum (admission 1d) was also extended and for the first time a catalogue of its contents was available, indicating that Belle Vue was now undertaking its own printing, although guide books were not regularly produced until 1856. A long, two-storey extension was added to the museum block. This contained a lofty tea room, 27 yards by 8 yards, at first floor level, where visitors could obtain hot water free of charge. Beneath were five new animal dens, housing four young lions, costing £150, a Bactrian camel (£55) and a hyena. A consignment of several hundred young birds was bought from a Captain Miller, who had acquired them from a French vessel from Senegal. One of the lions died in October, poisoned by a rat catcher.

Apart from the musical contests, attractions for 1854 included a balloon ascent by Lieutenant Chambers on 5th July. He descended at Denton fifty minutes later, without mishap. He repeated his ascent, in an unusual wall-sided balloon named Victory, twice in August and twice in September (landing at Withington, Hattersley and Moston). On 25th September a Mr Dean made an ascent in a balloon named The Prince of Wales. In August, Professors Ransom and Hull took portraits in the centre of the Maze with their new American Daguerrotype apparatus. The firework display on 7th May was marred when the "signal gun" burst, causing two women to suffer broken legs.

The artists' room under the firework stand was extended in 1855 to form a saloon, 60 yards by 17 yards, capable of holding 5,000. The adjoining dancing platform now extended to half an acre. A new covered avenue, 200 yards long, was provided at the side of the sprint track, allowing visitors to view the occupants of the paddock in wet weather. There is no mention of the swimming baths (of 1852) in the 1855 rate valuation; these had not been a success and were now disused. An extra bear pit, adjacent to the first, was provided.

Attractions for 1855 included Prize Glee Singing, Spanish Minstrels and Senora Marrietta with her eight vocalists. An annual hand-bell ringing contest was introduced, lasting seven hours, and fifteen bands entered the brass band contest. The first prize was increased to £25, together with an E flat bombardon, mounted in German silver and valued at ten guineas. This year, bands were permitted to play only one piece of their own choice; the other was the test piece "Orynthia", composed for the contest by Mr Melling. The Harden Mills Band, from Bingley, were disqualified because they did not practise the test piece for the required four months and the band included non-bona-fide members for the contest.

1856 saw the opening of the great Music Hall under the firework stand. This had a floor area of over 27,000 square feet and could hold 10,000 people. It was constructed entirely of wood and was used for a concert by Madame Bernhardi and Signor Albicini on 3rd May. Refreshments could be served from various ancillary rooms, releasing the Tea Room, built in 1854, for use as a

ZOOLOGICAL GARDENS, BELLE VUE, MANCHESTER.—JULLIEN'S GRAND CONCERTS, THIS DAY, July 4, and Wednesday, July 8, 1857, with his Double Military Band, in addition to the following eminent solo performers: Oboe—M. Lavigne; Flute and Flageolet—MM. Mortieux and Collinet; Clarinet—Herr Sonnenberg; Trombones—Mr. Hawkes and M. Richir; Trumpet—M. Duhem; Fagotti—Mr. Hardy and M. Morlighem; E flat Clarinet—M. de la Fosse; Horns—Mr. Jarrett and M. Simar; Sax Ophicleide and Bombardon—M. Leray and Herr Jamaer; Ophicleide—Mr. Hughes; Cornet-à-pistons—Herr Kœnig; Pastoral Tibia—Picco; Vocalists—Misses Brougham.
Conductor..........M. JULLIEN.

PROGRAMME FOR THIS DAY.

Concert to commence at half-past six o'clock.

PART I.

Overture.........."Fra Diavolo"..........Auber.
New Quadrille.........."The English Lancers"..........Jullien.
(With solos by MM. Collinet, Mortieux, Lavigne, Hughes, Duhem, and Herr Kœnig.)
Symphony.."Andante from the Symphony in C Minor..Beethoven.
Song—Miss J. Brougham.."La Manola"..........Henrion.
Valse.........."The Gassier"..........Venzona.
(Dedicated to the celebrated soprano.)
Fantasia, Pastoral Tibia — Picco — On airs from Bellini's opera, "Norma"..........Bellini.
Duo—The Misses Brougham.."The Cousins"..........G. W. Glover.
New Galop.........."The Great Comet"..........Jullien.
(A descriptive Morceau de circonstance.)
Classic and Romantic — Dramatic and Melodramatic — Astronomic and Pyrotechnic—Eclectic and Empiric—Terrific and Comic.

PART II.

Grand Operatic Selection from Verdi's Opera, LA TRAVIATA.

(With solos for oboe, ophicleide, and cornets, performed by MM. Lavigne, Hughes, Duhem, and Kœnig.)
Prelude..........By the Orchestra.
Scena.........."Ah! was it he?"..........Verdi.
(Performed on the oboe, by M. Lavigne.)
Air.........."Let me bask in ev'ry pleasure"..........Verdi.
Air.........."From Provence, sea and land"..........Verdi.
(Performed on the ophicleide by M. Hughes.)
Recitative.........."Thus drink we"..........Verdi.
(Cornet-à-pistons, Herr Kœnig.)
Brindisi.........."We'll drink to the beauty"..........Verdi.
(Cornet-à-pistons and ophicleide, M. Duhem and Mr. Hughes.)
Polka.........."Minnie"..........Jullien.
Solo, Paganini's celebrated "Carnaval de Venise," performed on the Pastoral Tibia, Picco.
Duo—The Misses Brougham, "The Swiss Maidens"....W. H. Holmes.
Quadrille.........."Hibernian"..........Jullien.
Quick Step..........Kœnig.
Grand Finale......"God Save the Queen"....By M. Jullien's Band, the Band of the 4th Dragoons, and the Band of the Gardens.

In the evening, after the concert, Danson and Sons' Grand Representation of the SIEGE OF GIBRALTAR, with Double Display of Fireworks, by Bruce.

Tickets for Wednesday's concert, 1s. each, may be purchased up to Tuesday, at Messrs. Hime and Addison's, St. Ann's Square, and at the Gardens. Admission at the gates, on the concert days, 2s.—N.B. The tickets will be of two descriptions, those purchased for today's concert will not be available for that of Wednesday.

Advertisement for one of M Jullien's concerts, July 1857

printing office; guide books were now issued regularly.

The zoological collection now included six lions, three "Crimean" camels and two rhinos. There was a total of seven refreshment rooms in the Gardens, capable of seating between 100 and 1,000. There was also a Vinery and an Archery Ground. MacEwen's omnibuses ran from Brown Street in Manchester and along Stockport Road every fifteen minutes, excluding Sundays, at a fare of 3d inside, 2d outside. As yet there was no bus service along Hyde Road, except on gala days.

In 1858 Jennison leased the triangular area at the junction of Hyde Road and Kirkmanshulme Lane which he had been forced to give up in 1842. He immediately excavated a large lake, thereafter called the Great or New Lake. The Music Hall was extended and Danson painted frescos on its panelled ceilings. His subjects included the five previous firework pictures, together with numerous allegorical groups "illustrative of science, poetry and the arts". The exotic plant houses were extended and by the following year a total of thirty pleasure boats had been provided on the two lakes.

On 7th July, celebrated aeronaut Henry Coxwell ascended in his balloon "Queen". He took with him Mr Walker, of a Stockport firm of solicitors, and they descended at Gee Cross, near Hyde. Coxwell undertook four more trips before the end of August. Belle Vue saw its final balloon ascents on 9th and 14th July 1859. The aeronaut was a Mr Hall and he made his ascents wearing fancy dress and performing on a trapeze hanging from his balloon, the "Florence Nightingale".

There were two setbacks in 1859, although neither was permanent. The fireworks ("The Temple of Janus") were not a success as a battle scene had not been included and the visual effects were considered disappointing. Also, the Brass Band Contest was cancelled when only three bands entered. The popularity of the contests had declined since 1856, owing partly to events arranged elsewhere by Enderby Jackson.

In 1860 Jennison bought the leasehold of an area bounded by Kirkmanshulme Lane, Redgate Lane and The Avenue, which contained a large residence known as Kirkmanshulme House. In 1863 he bought the freehold of the site of the New Lake and in 1864 about 4½ acres of leasehold land between the railway at Longsight and Stockport Road. Family tradition maintains that Jennison made this purchase out of pride, in order to regain land which he had had to give up in 1842. For a more practical reason, he had bought a plot of land at Lees Street, Gorton, in 1856. Here he built seven cottages, one of which was turned into a beerhouse called the Garibaldi Inn.

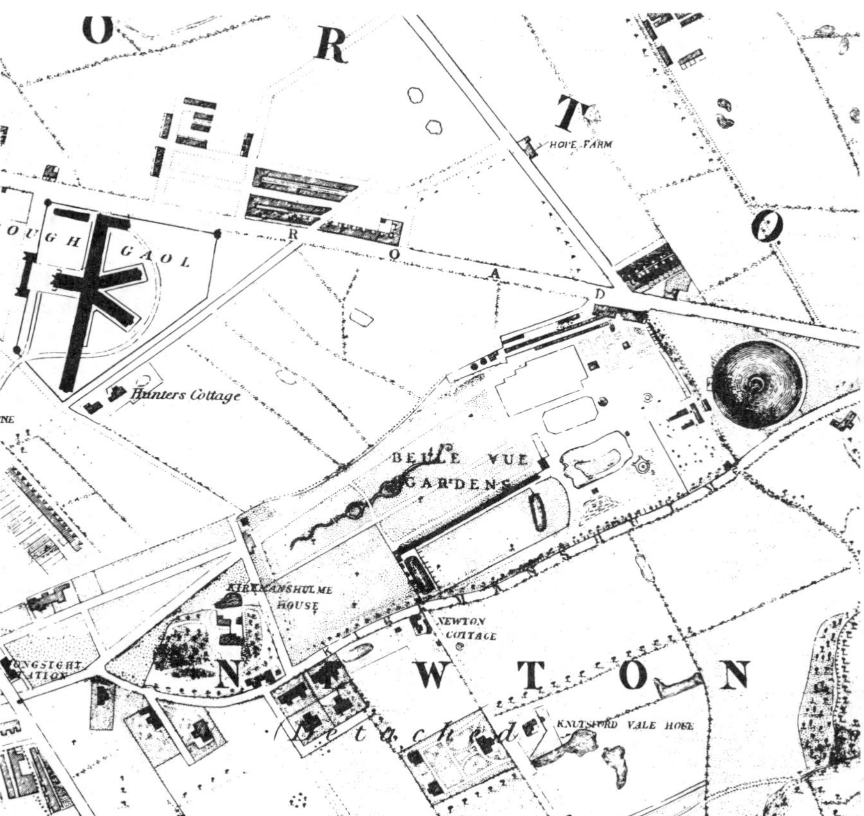

Part of Slater & Co's 1863 plan showing the Belle Vue or Borough Gaol and the Great Lake in its original circular shape

The Brass Band Contest resumed in 1861 in the Music Hall. Ten bands attended, including the London Victoria Amateurs, the first band from the South. There was a record Whit Monday, with 30,000 Eccles cakes, 10,000 buns, 1,000 meat pies and 100 hams being consumed. In June, Mr H Nadolski exhibited his "wonderful cabinet, 4½ft high, 3ft wide, 2ft deep, containing 200 articles of furniture", his demonstrations being preceded by "Tyrolese minstrels singing popular melodies". An elephant was acquired for £270, but died soon afterwards. The first tiger was obtained - the "King of Oudh's Fighting Tiger", said to be one of the spoils of the Indian Mutiny.

By 1862 there were two steamers on the New Lake, which was enlarged that year. An additional "spacious and lofty refreshment room", capable of seating 1,000, was erected (the Lighthouse bar and cafe of later years) and a new Monkey House was built. The latter was on the site of the old Cockatoo House and contained a large central cage and eight smaller ones. 1862 also saw a change in the firework arrangements. Until then, fireworks had been made in the Gardens by the contractor, Mr Bruce. This gentleman was dismissed in 1862 after an argument with Jennison, who gave his son James the job of making the fireworks. James had little knowledge of this and the year's display suffered. However, in time he acquired the necessary expertise.

Yet more boats were placed on the New Lake in 1863 and a set of steam hobby horses was placed to the left of the Hyde Road entrance, near the New Lake. Close to this, work had started on a large aviary, although the diminution in trade brought about by the American Civil War meant that its completion was delayed until 1866. A puma gave birth to four cubs, said to be the first such birth in this country.

The firework stand was roofed over in 1864 and the bandstand created in its centre, replacing the Arabesque Orchestra. A Hot Water Room, capable of seating 7,000, was provided at the Longsight end of the Music

The cottages on Lees Street built by John Jennison in 1856, photographed after the Garibaldi Inn had been sold to Allsopp's Brewery in 1928. By that time the beerhouse had been extended to occupy two of the cottages

Hall. In here, visitors could eat their own food at tables laid out with Belle Vue plates and cutlery. The Vinery was now located at the Longsight end and the Kitchen Garden, which previously adjoined Kirkmanshulme Lane, was now on the strip of land between The Avenue and the westerly boundary. Brick margins were provided for the two main lakes and the two entrances were connected by telegraph. An unusual attraction in the zoological collection was a hen living in the same cage as a Scottish terrier and its two pups. The Brass Band Contest attracted fifteen bands and an audience of 25,000, the best to date. The drum and fife competitions were discontinued.

John Jennison with six of his sons and daughter Ann, photographed in the 1860s

The Aviary, which incorporated a compartment for lions, and a pelican house were completed in 1866. The residue of the race-ground, where rabbit coursing seems to have ended about twelve years earlier, was laid out with serpentine walks and new, raised flower beds, representing a considerable extension to the Gardens. A further small lake for waterfowl was provided and the old paddock area opened out. More greenhouses were erected and another steamer, the Little Eastern, placed on the large lake. A large ice house was erected to complement a smaller one built in 1861.

On the firework island, a tower was built to resemble the round tower of Windsor Castle. This held 50,000 gallons of water, used for special effects in the displays. The water was raised in twelve hours by two steam engines from a pit 70ft deep. Extra rooms adjacent to the Music Hall were opened, containing nine 32ft-long paintings by Danson of the French and Italian Alps, together with fourteen vignettes of English scenes. By now the Denton Omnibus Company was running a service along Hyde Road every $1\frac{1}{4}$ hours and the Manchester Carriage Company's service along Stockport Road was every ten minutes.

A new Fernery, adjacent to the Aviary, was opened in 1867. In the various refreshment rooms, tea or coffee could be obtained for 3d; veal pies 3d, ginger beer 2d a bottle, a plate of ham or beef 4d, Havana cigars 3d, 4d or 6d each. In 1869 a young Indian elephant, Sally, was bought for £500. This was the most expensive animal purchase to date, as the collection had been valued at only £1,000 barely two years earlier. The "own choice" in the Brass Band Contest was discontinued that year.

The Death of John Jennison

In the later 1860s the administration of Belle Vue was dominated by Jennison's final illness. Since about 1866 he had been affected by a spreading cancer of the face; his nose was cut off in an attempt to halt the disease. He spent long periods at health resorts such as Torquay and Askern, near Doncaster, and affairs at the Gardens were carried on in his absence by his sons and eldest daughter. In 1867 Jennison's eldest son, John, was excluded from the Belle Vue succession after his wife made some tactless remarks about the appearance of his father's face. Although generously remunerated by his father and remaining friendly with the rest of the family, John took no further part in the administration of the Gardens.

Old John Jennison died in the afternoon of 20th September 1869 and was buried in an imposing tomb in Cheadle Churchyard, which remains to this day. John Jennison had had a determination to succeed and a dislike of injustice, whether as persecutor or victim, and he had been capable of turning round every setback he suffered in the establishing of his Gardens. His capacity for innovation was legendary and it is said that his mottos were "Do it yourself" and "Novelty, always novelty". One of the Manchester newspapers had some years earlier described Belle Vue *"as a place of entertainment and amusement...one of the most remarkable institutions of which Manchester, or indeed any other city or town in the kingdom, can boast"*.

What finer accolade could be bestowed on the achievements of the previous forty years?

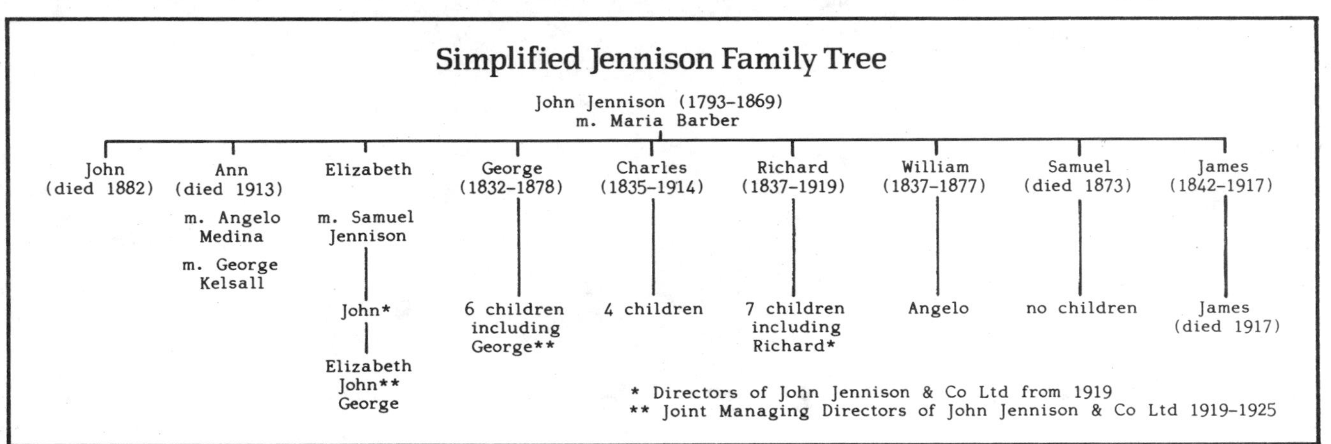

PROSPERITY UNDER THE FAMILY 1869-94

Before his death, John Jennison settled control of Belle Vue on his sons, George, Charles, James and Richard, and his eldest daughter, Ann. They were to hold the proceeds of the business in trust for themselves, the other sons, William and Samuel, and his grandson, John, son of his other daughter, Elizabeth. She had married a distant relative, another Samuel Jennison, from Bulwell. Samuel Jennison, the son, died in 1873 and William in 1877. Ann, who had remarried George Kelsall on the death of her first husband, Angelo Medina, was persuaded to relinquish her share of the Gardens in 1870 for an annuity of £400 and £1,000 at her death. Her new husband was apparently regarded as an undesirable pryer into family affairs.

The Administration of the Gardens under the Family

Most of the work in the 1870s fell on the shoulders of George, who had been his father's right hand man for the previous twenty years. All the managerial and clerical work was undertaken by the four brothers. No clerks were employed, although other staff had access to the offices in Belle Vue House. To keep financial affairs confidential to the family, the weekly expenditure and income sheets were drawn up with a crude code for the various parts of the site: M for Museum, Z for Maze, A for Hyde Road entrance, HWB for Hot Water Bar, etc. Sheets were used to record the weather, on which business depended, attendance and other information. The entry for Monday, September 7th 1874 records, "Dull and slight rain occasionally after 4pm". That for Monday, 1st September 1891 records, "All rooms very full, managed very well on the whole, rather short of bread and butter, had 1,000 loaves cut, 15,000 pies".

Outsiders had a significant role in the organisation of the musical contests, however. From 1863 the Brass Band contests had been entrusted to the Parker family, and they remained so for three generations. The Belle Vue enterprise assumed the title John Jennison & Co, and the close working together of the family enabled arrangements to be devised to combat such things as fraud at the turnstiles. The family also undertook outside catering; for some years John Jennison had transported a number of the Belle Vue staff to Wimbledon each year to provide refreshments at the National Rifle Association Championships. The hiring out of cutlery and crockery, even a temporary ballroom, were within the family's capacity.

The day-to-day requirements of the Gardens were considerable, ranging from building materials like broken stone, lime and thermoplastic putty, to "200 half cases of currants", casks of "Best Jamaica Ginger", bottles of soda water and lemonade for the refreshment rooms.

The family was always careful about detail. For example, on 28th March 1871 Mrs Butterworth of Downing Street, Ardwick, was instructed that "the ornament of the cake should not exceed 30/- in value", and in the same month both the Beverley Iron Company and the North Eastern Railway were taken to task over a grass mower damaged in transit.

The family employed a large workforce; in 1876 a total of 196 is recorded and the average wage was £1 per week. Many casual staff were taken on, particularly in the refreshment rooms, where women were paid between 2/6d and 5/- per week in the 1870s. Shawls, dresses, jackets and even bonnets were provided, often at costs vastly in excess of the average weekly wage. Even members of the family were employed on this basis - Hannah, Charles's wife, was on the payroll in 1871.

John Jennison had promoted a high degree of self-sufficiency in running the Gardens and this continued during the remaining years of family control. Most building work was undertaken "in house", although Thomas Bates & Sons of Droylsden Saw Mills did some work, and in particular laid a sewer between the Longsight entrance and Stockport Road in 1869. When the same firm built a shop and two houses fronting Kirkmanshulme Lane in 1867 and 1869, on the land bought in 1860,

George Jennison with his wife and children in 1876. His son, George, took over control of Belle Vue in 1919

common bricks, sand and lime were provided by Jennison. The bricks were baked from clay dug from the site of the Great Lake and from other land in the vicinity, bought or leased by the family. A total of 1,600,000 bricks was produced in 1853. There are also reports of bricks being hauled by elephant from the Harwood Road brickworks in Heaton Mersey.

Belle Vue achieved near self-sufficiency in other respects. Jennison brewed his own beer, particularly ginger beer, from an early date, and a new brewery with a capacity of 5,000 barrels was built near Hyde Road in 1872. A honey-combed cellarage linked the Music Hall with the Hyde Road entrance.

Pots and pans were made by the Gardens' own tinners and braziers, and coopers were employed to make tubs, baskets, barrels and buckets. A smithy, by the 1870s located to the left of the main entrance, had been in operation since the 1840s. The ashes and cinders from the smithy, gasworks and bakery were used in making up the internal paths and roadways. The Gardens had their own gas supply, and since about 1863 they had been supplying gas to some of Kirkmanshulme's public lamps. Vegetables were grown in the Kitchen Garden and lettuce and watercress teas were regarded as Belle Vue's speciality. No space was wasted; in 1867 mustard and cress was grown on a mound of earth which hid two tons of gunpowder for the fireworks. Some of the land outside the boundary walls was used as pasture to obtain a supply of milk. When this became water-logged in winter, the ice was broken up and stored in the ice houses, together with that from the lakes and ponds. Some was sold to butchers and fish merchants, who queued up at the front entrance early in the mornings, and some made Belle Vue's infamous flavoured water ices. Considered delicious by visitors, these contained algae and other impurities which were responsible for many an upset stomach.

Land and Property Acquisition

The sons continued their father's policy of acquiring land. Twelve freehold acres adjoining Hyde Road, linking the site with the City Gaol, were bought in December 1869, followed by 15 acres on the south side of Kirkmanshulme Lane in 1872. Three plots of land adjoining Belle Vue Street were bought in 1872 and 1873, when the Jennisons seized the opportunity to block the then private street with a tollgate and collected the proceeds therefrom.

A seven-acre leasehold plot, on the southern side of the Kirkmanshulme Lane junction with Pink Bank Lane, was acquired for £1,000 in 1871. A 19-acre plot on the northern side of the same junction had been leased by old John, probably about 1844, as substitute pastureland when the initial extension of the Gardens took place. Over the years, this plot, the site of the present athletics facility, became known by the family as Firework Land, no doubt because large crowds of sightseers gathered there to watch the firework displays over the wall on Firework Island free of charge.

Sixteen acres on the western boundary, straddling Redgate Lane, were bought in 1874, and eleven houses on Norman Street and two houses on Vernon Street in the same year. In 1878 a plot of land was acquired on Mona Street, at its junction with Cambert Lane, on the north side of Hyde Road, on which were built eighteen houses. Another $2\frac{1}{2}$ acres were bought at the Longsight end of Kirkmanshulme Lane in 1882, on which were built six houses known as Victoria Terrace and three houses fronting Kirkmanshulme Lane called Wimbledon Terrace, no doubt after the Jennison connection with the Rifle Association events. Further purchases of land and houses off Pink Bank Lane, Kirkmanshulme Lane, Mount Road and Woodland Street were to be made in 1888, 1889, 1893, 1901 and 1904. The Midland Hotel, Hyde Road, next to Belle Vue Station, was bought in 1887 and became another outlet for the Jennison Brewery. By 1905 John Jennison and the family had bought 32 acres of land for incorporation into the Gardens, making a total of 68 acres within the walls. A further 42 freehold acres and 58 leasehold were acquired outside the walls.

The reasons for these purchases varied. In some cases there was a specific purpose; the 1872 Kirkmanshulme Lane acquisition, for example, was to establish a brickfield. The Victoria Terrace, Mona Street, Norman Street and Woodland Street purchases were for staff housing. The need to protect the environment of the Gardens from the encroaching industries of an ever-growing Manchester was another factor, as was the need to strengthen the family's hand against the day when the lease of the original Gardens expired and would have to be renegotiated.

Elephant in front of the Indian Grotto, photographed pre-1880

Much of the land was used for pasture, and members of the family lived in the three houses at Belle Vue Place and some cottages that came with the Pink Bank Lane lands. Adjacent to these cottages was a private sportsground for the Kirkmanshulme Cricket Club, which was no doubt another family-supported organisation. On the whole, all the acquisitions proved to be good investments as far as the Gardens were concerned, as they were used many years later for purposes quite unthought-of by the Jennisons, and proved a valuable source of capital income for the Company that was to take over the Gardens.

The Jennisons and Local Government

Most family members were active in local government, being represented at various times on County and Urban District Councils, as well as Manchester Corporation. These involvements benefited the Gardens and it is said that the drainage of surrounding areas was designed to empty into the Great Lake, which itself emptied into the smaller lakes and ponds. Although a permanent water supply was laid on later from the canal at Gorton Bridge, it is said that the value of the water received from street drainage was worth at least £1,000 per annum.

Firework Displays

The firework spectacle had continued to evolve since the 1850s. A wing was added to each side of the island in 1856. Each wing contained five moveable trucks, varying from 2ft to 12ft in width, on which were mounted sections of the Picture. These could be moved to alter the background during the display itself. The water tower served thirty hydrants, which were in use each night as the wooden floor always caught fire, despite being wetted before performances. A series of slopes in the rear of the island enabled marching columns, horses, camels and elephants to be paraded effectively. No insurance company would cover the spectacle and the family considered this a positive advantage. Accidents were infrequent, although a first-aid box was maintained in the actors' dressing room, supported by their own contributions. The actors tended to be the poor and unemployed of the neighbourhood and part of their payment was in beer and pies. The whole display lasted about twenty minutes. An explosion in the original firework shop at the Longsight entrance some time between 1862 and 1866 caused the removal of the firework manufactory to the old swimming baths building, where the central pond was considered useful from the safety point of view.

Expansion under George Jennison 1870-78

Under the direction of George, the 1870s saw a considerable number of developments which substantially increased the overall scale of the Gardens. The original two-acre garden attached to Belle Vue House had been transformed beyond recognition and the original seating arbours had gone, as had many of the statues. Their place was taken by an ornate Italian Garden, located between the Great and Picture Lakes, which adjoined a greenhouse containing camellias and orange trees. Nearby was a series of rustic grottos in the style of an Indian temple.

In the spring of 1870 a specially designed maze, the New Maze, was planted next to the two waterfowl lakes. Three years later there was a large piece of ornamental rockwork at its centre and, as with the earlier Hampton Court maze, admission was 1d. A free drinking fountain, supplied by one of the wells sunk in the Gardens, was erected near the waterfowl lakes in 1870. Adjacent to the steam hobby horses, a set of steam velocipedes was provided, described as "an early type of bicycle made of cast iron fixed to a round wooden platform which whizzed around at great speed". The Kitchen Gardens were further extended and towards the end of the year an Asiatic Kiosk, designed by Danson, was provided near the Longsight entrance to accommodate ostriches, emus, etc.

In 1871, four giraffes were purchased for the first time. In 1872 another elephant was bought for £680 on the break-up of Wombwell's Menagerie No.1 in Edinburgh. He was named Maharajah and achieved some notoriety when he came to be transported to Manchester. When placed in a railway cattle truck, he apparently lifted the roof off with his trunk. It was then decided to walk the animal all the way, accompanied by his keeper, Lorenzo. At one point on the journey, there was an argument at a tollgate over the correct toll payable for the elephant. Maharajah settled the matter by smashing through the obstruction. This incident, now considered to be a myth, was portrayed in a painting by Heywood Hardy called "The Disputed Toll".

Maharajah was an immediate success in the Gardens, and for the next ten years, before he died of pneumonia, he gave rides to visitors. In the Jennison tradition, however, he had to earn his keep. Apart from taking part in Whitsuntide and other processions through the streets of Manchester, there are reports of Maharajah grinding coffee and pulling carts of meat and bricks. In 1872, just inside the Hyde Road entrance, were built the new brewery and stabling for five

The Belle Vue Place houses, photographed in 1985 when they were semi-derelict

hundred horses. The walls of the Gardens were increased in height to 14 feet, buttressed with 9-inch brick pillars every 14 feet. The "free list visitors" had been a problem, for in the previous year the services of no fewer than seven police constables and one sergeant had been requested to patrol the grounds at one time.

1873 saw the enlargement of the Hyde Road entrance to the form it kept for many years. Another fernery was laid out near the Lion House. A "Photograph Room" was also provided, open daily in summer, although it does not appear to have been a success and had disappeared by 1877. New "breeding ponds" were laid out between The Avenue and the small waterfowl lakes. One of the occupants was a seal. An extensive "recreation lawn" was made near the Longsight entrance, and another Italian Garden and Ornamental Terrace off The Avenue. A Croquet Lawn also appeared. There was a new glass-roofed Elephant House for Maharajah and his companion, Sally. The following year a small glass Giraffe House was built near the range of cages in the former paddock area, originally constructed in 1852. The land next to the City Gaol, purchased in 1872, was used in 1874 for the Lancashire Agricultural Show. In the same year, alterations were made to the Brass Band contests; 24 players were now allowed in each band (two more than before) and "valve trombones" were banned.

"The Disputed Toll", showing Maharajah and Lorenzo arguing with the tollgate keeper

The first annual boat race on the Great Lake was held in 1875, and Captain Boyton demonstrated his life-saving dress in which he had crossed the Channel a few weeks earlier. In September 1875 trade received a further boost through the opening of Belle Vue Station on Hyde Road, 200 yards from the eastern extremity of the Gardens. The station was equipped with two bay platforms, one for each direction, to handle excursion traffic.

Over the winter, a new brick Elephant House was built adjoining the one put up in 1873, which had been a failure because the bars of the cages were too weak to contain the inmates. The new structure also accommodated a rhino and a hippo.

To take full advantage of the opening of Belle Vue Station, the Gardens were provided with a new entrance and hotel, the Lake Hotel, which opened on 31st July 1876. The Great Lake was also enlarged, now being pear-shaped instead of circular. Maharajah was used for the first time in the fireworks display, carrying "The Prince of Wales". The Lion House was extended, enabling the adjoining Aviary to expand. (In the guide books, the original Lion House (of 1866) had always been referred to as Aviary No.3.)

A Beaver Pond was laid out for 1877, near to the breeding ponds. Extensions were made to the Picture Lake and the Hampton Court Maze was repositioned and replanted. The small refreshment room in Maze Cottage was enlarged. Part of the Hyde Road wall was taken down and rebuilt to provide a coach and omnibus stand. The increasing urbanisation of the area was apparent through improved bus services - the Manchester Carriage Company maintained a five-minute frequency on Stockport Road and a fifteen-minute frequency on Hyde Road. (The latter was soon to become toll free.)

Finally for 1877, a lengthy railway siding to serve the gasworks and brewery was laid from the Longsight railway yard, across Redgate Lane and

A ticket office at the Great Lake, photographed in the late 1940s. The lake had been drained for cleaning

up the westerly boundary (since the 1869 and 1874 land purchases, Hunters Lane), following Hyde Road to terminate at two sidings near the brewery. This cost £750. The firework display that year was attended by the Lord Mayor of Manchester and the display included a representation of the new Town Hall on the night of his visit. The proceeds of the evening went to the Indian Famine Relief Fund.

In 1878 new cages were erected near the Giraffe House, and a range of cages for monkeys was added inside the Elephant House.

Richard Jennison in 1899, showing, according to George Jennison, "his natural pose".

Expansion under James 1878-94

George Jennison died in September 1878, at the early age of 46, and thereafter administration was divided between the three remaining brothers, albeit rather unequally. Charles concerned himself with the botanical side and with the legal relationships that the Gardens had with surrounding landowners. Richard preferred a more passive role, mixing with visitors and seeing to their wellbeing and enjoyment. He was accused of idleness in later years. Most of the work, especially in relation to the fireworks and the zoo, fell on James's shoulders. Members of his family later accused him of timidity in undertaking new ventures in the Gardens, but this does not appear justified.

Further extensions to the Lion and Tiger House were carried out over the winter of 1879/80. Tramways were opened along both Hyde and Stockport Roads by the Manchester Carriage & Tramways Company in May 1880, with a seven-minute and three-minute frequency respectively. The family arranged for a double track private siding to be laid on the coach and omnibus stand, which was used to stable horse trams taking visitors home after the firework displays.

The guide book for 1881 was the first since 1847 to contain a map and this was revised annually to keep abreast of alterations and developments. A new Confectionery Bar, a Ladies' Refreshment Room and Lavatory were erected on the banks of the Great Lake, near the Camellia and Orange House. A large new Camel and Dromedary House was built and a new Monkey House, in the style of an Indian temple or mosque, appeared on the site of the waterfowl lake of 1866. The building was designed by Mr B Firth, an employee, and it was kept to a temperature of 60°-70°F by a series of hot water pipes. Inside was a great central cage, with nine 12ft square cages on each side of the building. Apparatus to keep the inmates amused took the form of a "village pump and draw-well" (an elevator from which they could draw corn), a large wheel and a rocking horse. The existing octagonal Monkey House (of 1862) near what had become the Leopard House (beneath the Museum) now housed parrots. The Giraffe House had been dismantled as the attempt to keep these animals was not successful.

The Great Lake, further enlarged in 1882, now had a central island with clock tower, from which the half hour sessions for the hire of boats were timed. A cricket and archery ground had been laid out near the junction of Hunters Lane and Redgate Lane. During 1882, the Kirkmanshulme Cricket Club ground at the corner of Pink Bank Lane was used by the West Gorton St Mark's Amateur Football Club, which later became part of Ardwick FC, which in turn became Manchester City Football Club.

On 22nd June 1883 a celebration was held to commemorate the coming of age of Richard's son, Richard. Among the attractions

The Great Lake with its clock tower, from a drawing which appeared in guide books of the 1890s

were a cricket match, a hundred yards race for youths under 20, a sixty yards race for unmarried women, a pole jump for all comers, a tug of war, a wheel-barrow race and an egg-and-spoon race. "Comic and sentimental singing by amateurs" was also provided. The celebration ended with a firework display. Later in 1883, on the first Monday of October, a fire broke out about midnight on Firework Island, destroying half the picture.

A new Seal House, next to the Camel House, was built in 1885. Parts of Aviary No.1 were now used to house lions and other big cats. In this year the Gardens were provided with electricity, initially to light the bandstand. The generator was upstairs in the Music Hall block, near the Elephant House.

In 1886 the octagonal Parrot House, which had formerly held monkeys, was removed. A second brass band concert was introduced in July, for bands which had not gained prizes at the September contest for the previous four years. Over forty bands entered for this secondary contest in its first year, but public attendances, although good, did not equal those for the September contest. Success in July meant that a band was automatically invited back the following September. The Heywood Rifles Band carried off both prizes in 1886.

The cricket and archery ground adjacent to Hunters Lane was converted into an athletic ground in 1887 and the Salford Harriers began using it three times a year. For the next 25 years, the annual Manchester and Salford Schools' Sports Day was held on this ground. The same year saw the first Sunday concert in the Ballroom by the Gorton Philharmonic Society, of which the family were patrons. The concerts were called "open rehearsals" because the public were admitted free of charge. The orchestra was allowed to use the Gardens' facilities free of charge and was associated with Belle Vue for almost 89 years. In the same year, the original 1873 Elephant House was converted into a refreshment room called the First Class Cafe.

The guide book for 1888 advised the public that they could inspect the firework factory on application. The cages next to the factory, dating from the 1850s, were now enclosed and called the Paddock House. Nearby, a small Penguin House with an indoor glass tank had been erected. The Seal House had been transformed into the Sealion House and displays were given in its large pool, 64ft long, 20ft wide and 3ft deep - a very early instance of such aquatic displays in this country. The first keeper in charge of the displays rejoiced in the name Jack Cupid. The skeleton of Maharajah, who had died six years earlier, was now in the Museum and a large room for the distribution of hot water was located at the Longsight end of the Ballroom. The City Gaol was closed in 1888 and was demolished two years later.

A large-scale redecoration of the Music Hall (now called the Ballroom) was carried out in 1889, two of the larger tea rooms being painted in Chinese style. New regulations were brought into the Brass Band contests, including a requirement that the test pieces should not be played in public prior to the performance. A small collection of reptiles, including live crocodiles, was now on display in the Museum.

A set of cages for kangaroos was erected near the Elephant House in 1890 and the following year, near the New Maze, a range of cages was provided for prize pigeons lent by the Manchester Columbarian Society. Two years later, a pheasantry was placed next to the Penguin House.

Another of Wombwell's travelling menageries was dispersed in London in 1893 and in June a chimpanzee named Consul was obtained from the sale. Although he died of dropsy in November 1894, in his short time at the Gardens, Consul made a name for himself. Dressed in smoking

IN MEMORY OF

"CONSUL,"

The Belle Vue Chimpanzee, who died Nov. 24th, 1894,

AGED ABOUT 5 YEARS.

"Hadst thou a soul?" I've pondered o'er thy fate
Full many a time: Yet cannot truly state
The result of my ponderings. Thou hadst ways
In many things like ours. Then who says
Thou'rt not immortal? That no mortal knows,
Not e'en the wisest—he can but *suppose*.

'Tis God alone knows where the "Missing Link"
Is hidden from our sight; but, on the brink
Of that Eternal line where we must part
For ever, sundering heart from heart,
The truth shall be revealed: but not till then—
The curtain, raised by the Almighty, when
Mankind must answer for the deeds of men.

BEN BRIERLEY.

A memorial sheet to Consul I, printed by W E Clegg of Oldham and sold for one penny

jacket and cap, and puffing a cob pipe, he often attended business meetings with James Jennison. Consul had been so successful with visitors that a second chimpanzee was immediately obtained and named Consul II. His party trick was to play a violin whilst riding a tricycle. Later he rode a bicycle.

Another attraction introduced in 1893 was a Jungle Shooting Range, located to the left of the Hyde Road entrance near the Steam Horses and Velocipedes, in what must have looked like a small fairground. 1894 saw the introduction into this area of another amusement called the Ocean Wave. Identical to one shown at the Paris Exhibition that year, and a refinement of earlier "Sea on Land" amusements, this was described in the Manchester Weekly Times:

"...a circular platform, equipped like the bridge of a ship, is set among scenery painted to represent the waves of an ocean during a high wind. Round the edge of the platform is a line of small yachts. Powerful machinery makes the platform revolve, and at the same time rise and fall, giving the yachts a motion not unlike the ones they have at sea. A very popular form of entertainment, judging by the number who patronised it and their shrieks of laughter."

The Ocean Wave, a popular amusement of the late Jennison era

The Gardens in the 1890s

The early 1890s saw the zenith of Belle Vue's popularity under the Jennisons. Dancing was popular, the open-air platform being frequently packed with young couples. One observer said that dancing took place "without much stiffness". Affairs were more sedate amongst the panelled murals, large mirrors and heavily-upholstered seating of the Ballroom.

Catering for the masses was considered as important as ever, and from various points round the site the public could obtain tea or coffee for 3d a cup, ginger beer for 2d a bottle, lemonade for 3d a bottle, milk or cider for 2d a glass and buns and buttered biscuits for 1d each. 2d would purchase Eccles cakes, a plate salad or a round of ham or beef sandwiches. A veal pie cost 3d, whilst a plate of meat with bread and butter cost 9d. Bread, butter, biscuits and salad could be bought together for a shilling.

Rowing boat on the Small or Firework Lake, to the rear of Firework Island, 1907

Passengers on the three steamers, Little Britain and Little Eastern on the Great Lake and Favourite on the Firework Lake, were frequently subjected to falling specks of soot from the boats' smokestacks, whilst children in rowing boats could not resist the temptation to land on the central island of the Great Lake, frequently to be marooned when rival gangs stole their boats or oars. It took two children to handle each oar. In winter, the lakes saw skating or the Scottish sport of curling.

The scope of the zoological collection was considerable, although there were notable omissions, particularly giraffes, which were impossible to obtain because of troubles in the Sudan. Penguins were also in short supply because of an import ban, brought in when it was feared they were getting scarce. However, certain unusual species were represented, notably Pere David's deer, which were displayed in the Camel House towards the end of the decade. There was a large monkey collection, the Monkey House being one of the zoo's most popular areas. Many were acquired easily from sailors who brought the animals home as pets. This supply was fortunate, as no fewer than 150 monkeys died each year, owing mainly to the impossibility of keeping the Monkey House hot enough during the winter. Other animals died in cold weather, including the condors, whose feet tended to drop off despite the fact that the birds originate from the High Andes.

Certain lessons were learned over the years, one of which was that animals used to an outdoor life in summer did best if kept outdoors in winter. Thus kangaroos could stand tolerably cold weather and even the rhino was happy at a temperature of 50°F. The water in the pools of the Elephant House was allowed to freeze over without detriment to either elephant or rhino. Pumas were allowed to walk in the snow and the spotted hyena was found to prefer the open air to a heated compartment in winter.

The Gardens had their critics. Some of the events and attractions were seen by the perceptive for what they were - merely the means of attracting more visitors through the turnstiles. Many of the attractions were little different from the early days, and appeared pathetic compared to the band contests which were now reaching a high degree of sophistication. On the whole, the critics were in a minority.

THE LAST DECADES OF FAMILY CONTROL 1894-1925

Consolidation and the Influence of George Jennison 1894-1914

The post of scenic artist for the firework displays was taken over by Messrs Caney & Perkins and to commemorate the opening of the Manchester Ship Canal in 1894 a dual programme was arranged, combining "The Siege of Granada" with "Success to the Ship Canal".

In 1895 arrangements were made to obtain a small permanent water supply for the Great Lake from the canal one mile away at Gorton Bridge. The involvement of the Manchester Columbarian Society had ceased, although the pigeon cages were still present. In the spring, a new range of cages was erected adjoining the Camel and Giraffe House and used for the display of capybaras, cassowaries, etc.

"A Day at Belle Vue" (1894). The background scenery is for the firework display, "The Siege of Granada"

The next generation of Jennisons was brought increasingly into the running of the Gardens during the 1890s. George, educated at Pontefract and Balliol College, Oxford, where he read law, became a Fellow of the Zoological Society and introduced many progressive changes to the zoo. In 1895 he married a Swiss lady, Gabrielle Duccoroy. Another of the younger Jennisons worth mentioning is Angelo, one of the sons of the late William. He was named after Ann's first husband, Angelo Medina, a cornet player from Lecco in Italy who died in 1869. Angelo Jennison's interests in the Gardens were the development of its electrical system and running the brewery.

In 1897 the Hampton Court Maze was removed and a new generator building was erected on the site to supply the entire Gardens with electricity for arc and incandescent lights. Two engines (of 200hp and 80hp) were installed, but these were inadequate and two years later two 250hp Benjamin Goodfellow Corliss steam engines were provided to drive the dynamos.

Also provided in 1897 was a wooden building called the Kinematograph for the display of animated pictures. Located between the Camel and Elephant Houses, this was one of the earlier, if not the earliest, purpose-built cinemas in the country. In 1902 a continuous programme, operating every twenty minutes from 1.00pm to 4.30pm, showed film of the Coronation of King Edward VII.

The Great Lake was the scene of a fatality in 1897, when a girl drowned underneath a rowing boat. A Tobacco Divan was erected near the lake and in 1898 a "present store" was built at the same location. An area of ornamental rockwork was laid out near the New Maze for mountain species.

The September Brass Band Contest of 1898 was attended by John Henry Iles, who was to return, a quarter of a century later, as the managing director of Belle Vue. Iles originated from Bristol and had succeeded to his father's timber business at the age of 17. He was an organist and pianist, and whilst in London on business was induced to take over the ailing publication, "Organist and Choirmaster", turning round its fortunes overnight. During a visit to Manchester, he asked a porter at the Midland Hotel what was worth seeing. The porter directed him to the Belle Vue contest and Iles at once became interested in the brass band world. On returning to London, Iles acquired the publication "British Bandsman" and the band music publishers, R Smith & Co. Two years later, with Sir Arthur Sullivan, Iles organised the National Brass Band Contest at the Crystal Palace.

In 1899 an open air pool for sealions was provided next to the Sealion House. An orang-utan, "The Wild Man of

Borneo", was acquired for £150 and kept in the Lion House. Although the animal lived only six weeks, the purchase was successful in terms of the number of people who thronged the building. At one stage, six policemen had to be called to control the crowds.

In November 1899 a Torchlight Tattoo and Sham Fight was put on by various Corps of Volunteers in aid of the Boer War Fund. A series of Military Band contests was initiated in 1900, and in 1903 a series of Choral competitions began. The Great Ballroom had been renovated and contained paintings by Caney.

A Band Contest in the 1890s. Until 1929, these were held in the Ballroom

The Gardens closed on the day of Queen Victoria's funeral, a gesture which was not copied by Belle Vue's competitors. Hexagonal enclosures for wolves and foxes were laid out at the rear of the Maze and the Museum was now referred to as the Reptile House, because of the large number of live specimens it contained.

In 1902 there was a "recently enlarged Model Room, containing the latest automatic novelties" between the Ballroom and the Printing Office. Important additions were made to the zoo, including specimens of giant Galapagos and Aldabra land tortoises loaned by the Hon. Walter Rothschild, MP, of Tring. On George Jennison's instructions, the winter temperature of the Monkey House was reduced and some windows removed, resulting in a decreased death toll from tuberculosis. Flamingos, storks and herons now had an extensive open enclosure, and in other open air enclosures, efforts were made to introduce a natural appearance through the placing of trees, plants and rocks. An open air lion cage was proposed, and after it had been placed outside, the spotted hyena ceased its habit of progressively eating itself!

Manchester Corporation introduced electric trams along Hyde and Stockport Roads, the former beginning on 1st June. The fare was 2d inside or outside. The old horse tram sidings fell out of use. The Corporation also wanted to lay a circular route along Belle Vue Street and Kirkmanshulme Lane, including a lengthy siding at the northern end of the latter. Negotiations for additional land for the Kirkmanshulme Lane route had been initiated as early as 1896, but dealings only began in earnest in 1902. The Jennisons were prepared to allow the siding, provided that it was used only for the firework traffic, could be discontinued by them at one week's notice and could be removed by them if it fell out of use.

Not unnaturally, the Corporation considered these terms onerous, but a compromise was worked out and an eight-minute service was using Kirkmanshulme Lane from Easter Monday 1903, terminating at Belle Vue. In the case of Belle Vue Street, agreement was not so easy, as this was a private street where the family had a tollgate. The Corporation sought compulsory powers, but in 1904 the Jennisons appealed to the House of Lords against the Corporation's Bill. By May that year a settlement was reached and the Corporation got possession of the land on 1st June. The trams first ran on 23rd July and the full circular service began on 21st November 1904. Two further tramway sidings were provided by the Corporation on land leased from the family in Mount Road in August 1905. The part played by Charles Jennison, by now a Conservative member of

Pelicans inside Bird of Prey Terrace

the City Council, was a crucial one in these negotiations.

In 1903 a large glass-fronted enclosure was provided in the Elephant House, containing ferns and other plants, lizards and Mr Rothschild's tortoises. A large snake cage, 70ft long by 12ft high, was provided in the Camellia and Orange House. A cast of 400 took part in the firework display of that year, "The Capture of Gibraltar".

Giraffes were added again in 1904, kept in the Camel House. Hussain the Indian Juggler and Necromancer appeared as an attraction for the season. New refreshment rooms were opened in the Ballroom block and one, the Chinese Cafe and Smoke Room, was a redecoration of a previous refreshment room.

In 1905 a Monster Troupe of Wild Animals, comprising young lions, leopards, wolves, polar Russian and Japanese bears, borrowed from the world renowned Carl Hagenbeck, were used in frequent exhibitions of "how wild animals are trained" in a giant open air cage.

1906 saw the installation of an outdoor tank next to the Elephant House, for the use of elephants. The "Helter Skelter Lighthouse - a Light Delight" was located on the banks of the Picture Lake, near the electrical installation. A series of dance competitions and humorous singing contests was arranged in the Ballroom. The winners of the latter were sometimes judged by the amount of applause they received.

The Manchester Motor Car Show was held between 8th and 18th February 1907. Stricter rules were drawn up to regulate the Brass Band competitions. One rule prevented any band from winning the contest more than three years in succession. Any such bands could not compete the following year, but received a gold medal instead. Members of bands had to live within four miles of the town where their band was based, and other rules governed the use of professional players and prevented the transfer of players between bands.

Three new amusement features were introduced in 1908. A Faery Glen was provided at the Great Lake, designed by Mr R Caney. Near the Waterfowl Lake and the Helter Skelter Lighthouse, a Pagoda marked the entrance to Laughter Land, which included a hall of mirrors and an amusement arcade. Finally, the Figure Eight Toboggan, a small-scale version of the scenic railway, was placed between the Maze and Paddock House. This novelty was introduced after James Jennison had seen one displayed at the White City, Stretford. At the July Brass Band Competition, the Upper Norwood Road Band from London appeared in uniform, the first time this had happened.

The Polar Bear Enclosure with the two bear pits in the background

The Gardens closed on the day of Edward VII's funeral in 1910, the lost takings estimated at over £2,000. Again, other establishments did not follow suit. The Kings Hall, suitable for "Demonstrations, Exhibitions, Social Gatherings, etc", was built in a period of six weeks. The name commemorated the two kings in whose reigns it was constructed. The Hot Water Room was moved to the back of the new building, enabling the old area to be laid out with a 200ft-long maple floor for use as a roller skating rink. Admission was free, although the hire of skates was 6d per session.

The July Brass Band Contest was split up into three sections; twenty bands took part in the July contest and eighteen in a new contest for beginners in May. Prior to this there had been some 30-50 bands applying to play in the July contest and it was feared that entries would fall off because of the

The Chinese Cafe, where some of Belle Vue's higher class clientele dined during the Jennison era

constant discouragement of failing to get a place. From now on, it would take a new band three years to earn a place at the September contest.

In 1910 calcium carbide, used in "The Battle of Manchester" firework display, exploded and a fireman died. A new pool for crocodiles and alligators was provided in the Camellia and Orange House in 1911, and a year later the Kinematograph was converted to an Anthropoid Ape House at the suggestion of George Jennison. Its three new cages were filled with orang-utans.

On the first day of 1914 an aircraft exhibition opened at Belle Vue and Mr B C Hucks took off from Belle Vue's athletic ground in a Bleriot Tornado aircraft and looped the loop four times. Three days later Hucks took off for Leeds, but his journey had to be terminated when he ran into a snowstorm. In May, Charles Jennison died.

Mr B C Hucks in his Bleriot monoplane. photographed at Belle Vue on 1st January 1914

The Great War

At the outbreak of war the family allowed the Government to use parts of the grounds for military purposes free of charge. The Manchester Regiment drilled in the Gardens, and the Kings Hall and skating rink were put to use for making aircraft parts and training workers for aircraft manufacture at the Government factory at Heaton Chapel. In 1915, on the south side of the athletic ground, a long building was erected with railway sidings for the manufacture of munitions. This building was visited by King George V and it must have irritated the family's sense of patriotism when he did not visit the rest of Belle Vue, which remained open to the public. George Jennison served as a foreman in the munitions factory.

Many of the animal keepers volunteered for the services and women were appointed in their place. Difficulties were encountered in replacing animal losses and certain foodstuffs were hard to obtain. The firework displays continued almost as normal, but the use of rockets was prohibited under the Defence of the Realm Act. The displays were contemporary in their subject matter, that for 1915 being entitled "The Battle of the Marne", for 1916 "The War in Flanders" and for 1918 "The Fight for Liberty". It is reported that during one of the shows a spectator became so incensed that he splashed across the Picture Lake to join in the "fighting".

The display for 1917 was seriously affected by a fire which broke out among some uniforms in the dressing room. The blaze was fanned by the wind with the result that all the uniforms were destroyed, together with a large part of the Picture. The then scenic artist, Bernard Hastain, had just joined the army and he was given a special two-week leave of absence to help rectify the disaster. The displays continued for the rest of the season, although many of the players wore only old uniforms and others just a uniform cap. Prior to joining up, Hastain had designed an Aladdin's Cave on the rear part of the Firework Lake, later known as the River Caves and later still as the Chinese Grotto.

Sir James de Hoghton inspecting National Volunteers at Belle Vue on Saturday April 29th 1916. The Kings Hall is in the background

Although interest in the Brass Band contests declined during the war, in 1915 a series of concertina contests was started. The same year, the family took the opportunity to secure their long term interests by purchasing the freehold of the original 35¼ acres for £35,000. They also bought the freehold of the "firework land" on Kirkmanshulme Lane and negotiated longer term leases of Kirkmanshulme House and the land bordering Belle Vue Avenue.

As the war progressed, the military use of the site became more intensive and at one time the public was only admitted at weekends. In the autumn of 1917 George Jennison made a number of suggestions to James about the improvement and development of the Gardens.

These included altering the appearance of the Ballroom block, which was thought to be unsightly, removing greenhouses from the old westerly boundary in order that the munition factory could be incorporated in the Gardens at the war's end, altering the style of the firework displays, altering the main entrance, providing side shows and illuminations, trying out a circus at Christmas and variety shows in the summer, putting on boxing contests, developing exhibitions and obtaining a supply of electricity from Manchester Corporation to supplement their own supply.

Unfortunately James, who had been affected by the loss of his only son at Passchendaele earlier in the year, died in December before the proposals could be considered. Nor were they considered by Richard, the surviving son of the founder, for by now family bickering was taking place. The trouble had been brewing since 1895, when George and other members of the family proposed setting up a limited company to run the Gardens. This idea was always opposed by Richard who, it is said, was wealthy enough to buy out the rest of the family at any time. The others were not willing to allow this, as they considered that Richard had taken to "idle pursuits" and was not capable of running the Gardens.

The quarrel was finally settled when Richard died in 1919. John Jennison & Co Ltd was formed with a capital of £253,000, including bank loans and investments of £63,000. George Jennison was Chairman, Secretary, Treasurer and Joint Managing Director with John Jennison junior (old John's great grandson). John, William, Angelo and Richard Jennison junior took enough shares to qualify as directors. It was described as a "very happy Board with few meetings and an entire absence of quarrels".

Keepers with young chimpanzees and orang utan. "Monkey Terrace" is in the background

The Last Years of Family Control

With the end of the war, normality slowly returned to the Gardens. The munitions factory was handed over by the Government, became an exhibition hall and in November 1919 a large peace celebration was held in the building. The cages of the Zoo began to fill again, and additions included a hippo, zebra, dromedary and some monkeys originally bought by the Government for experiments with poisoned gas. An Indian elephant, named Lil, and a kookaburra were acquired in 1921 and the following year Frank, a large brown bear, arrived. He was to win the title "Father of the Zoo" before he died forty years later. Together with Lil came Phil Fernandez, a Malayan, who was a familiar and favourite sight in the Gardens for the next 35 years.

George Jennison was now given a free hand with the ideas for the Zoo. The Monkey House was provided with open air cages, where it is said the inmates' lives were extended fourfold. An experiment was tried with a pair of blue Himalayan magpies who had fought and had to be separated. After the removal of his mate, the male lost interest in himself until a mirror was placed in the cage, whereupon he immediately recovered.

The scope for large scale improvements to the Gardens was limited by the economic conditions of the time. Although 1919 and 1920 had been good years, labour costs were high and profits were minimal. Many of the buildings began to look dilapidated. No employees lost their jobs, although eight men were dismissed for stealing cash, resulting in a saving of £1,000 per annum. In 1920 and 1921 negotiations were held with Manchester City Football Club, who were looking for a new site to replace their ground on Hyde Road, after the main stand had been destroyed by

Boating on the lake, with the steamer "Favourite", in the early 1920s

fire. The athletic ground offered was considered too small, the family was unwilling to grant more than a 50-year lease, so the club moved to its Maine Road ground in 1923.

1922 saw the addition of a Junior section to the May Brass Band contests. In the September contest, the Besses o'th'Barn Band played in a concert formation, as opposed to the customary square. This change was universally followed after a few years. In 1924 a loudspeaker system was used to relay the September contest to members of the public who could not gain admittance to the Ballroom. In the same year a speech by Lloyd George was broadcast from the Kings Hall to an overflow audience.

The Kings Hall was not used very much in the 1920s, although the component parts of the Picture were painted there every spring. One of George Jennison's suggestions, a Christmas circus, was tried in 1922 but was not a success. Some exhibitions were held, such as the Manchester Dog Show, the Manchester Pigeon Society's Show and the National Fruit Show. The last named was soon moved to the Exhibition Hall. Lack of money prevented the implementation of many of George's suggestions, although the greenhouses were moved, a sideshow tried near the Ballroom an an attraction named Over the Falls was erected adjacent to the Paddock House. (Many of the suggestions were eventually accepted by the company which acquired the Gardens in 1925.)

Redgate Lane was made up into a public highway by Manchester Corporation in 1924 and it was proposed to run trams along it, although this did not happen. The same year there was a BBC outside broadcast, featuring the fireworks display, with George Jennison acting as commentator. It was followed by an attempt to get some animals to perform, apparently without much success.

The Sale of the Gardens

Rumours about the possibility of the Gardens being sold began circulating late in 1924. On 27th November an agreement was entered into between the Company and Harry George Skipp of London for the sale of the Gardens for £250,000. Whether Skipp was a genuine purchaser, a dealer or an intermediary is not known, but on 6th March 1925 another agreement was made between John Jennison & Co Ltd, Skipp and a new company, Belle Vue (Manchester) Ltd. The family was to take £89,500 of the purchase price in second mortgage debentures. A further £60,500 was invested by the family in the new company in first mortgage debentures. Management of the Gardens and other lands was vested in the new company from 1st January 1925, although formal transfer did not take place until 28th March. George Jennison was to act as zoological adviser for one year at a salary of £1,000 and John Jennison junior remained as electrical engineer and catering manager. The new company was prohibited from using the name Jennison in connection with the Gardens.

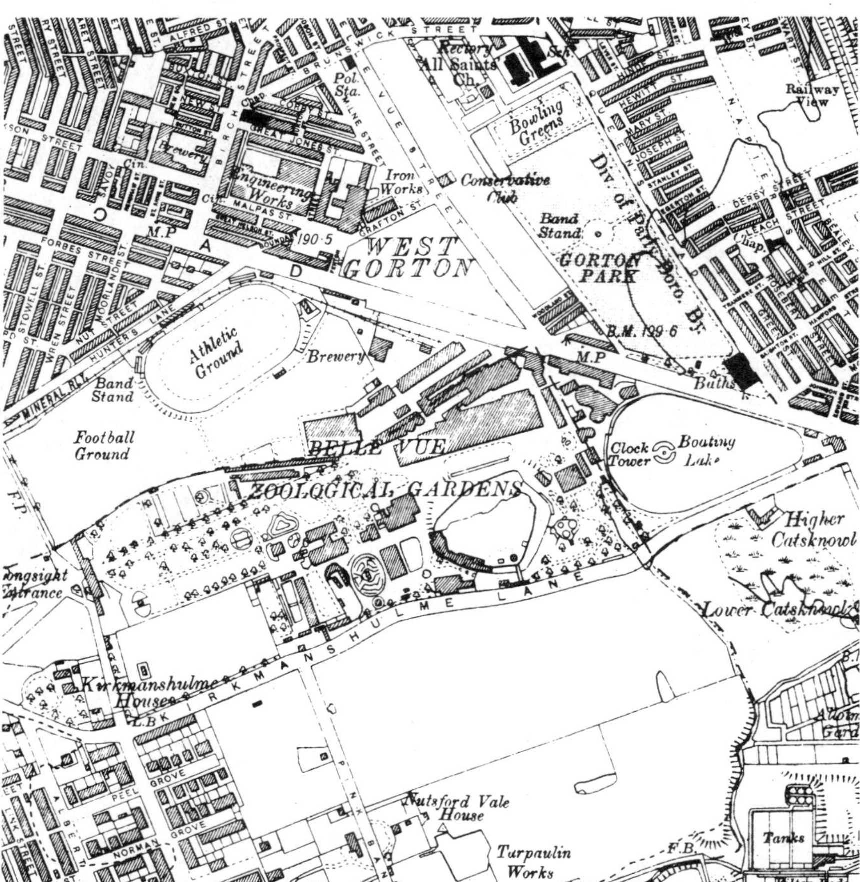

Ordnance Survey plan from the early 1920s, showing the site layout prior to the takeover by the Belle Vue Company

The sale had been brought about by George, who was anxious that secure arrangements be made to allow the continued development of the Gardens. He himself wished to devote time to other pursuits whilst he was still fit to do so. Although his own family was wealthy, he was disappointed in not having a son to whom he could have passed on the business, and his daughters had no interest in the Gardens. James's only son had been killed in 1917 and Charles had had only daughters, who had been estranged from him. Richard's children had the necessary capital to continue, but in George's eyes they lacked the inclination to take up what was required, and in any case, were in agreement with the sale. John Jennison junior, alone in opposition, did not have the means to finance the undertaking, and was therefore outvoted by the other directors.

The Gardens had been undergoing a slow decline since the peak of their success in the early 1890s, and the Great War and the troubled economic conditions of the early 1920s did not help. It was apparent that a radical change of direction and a great deal of investment were required if the Gardens were to continue in existence. Both these ingredients were provided by the new company. Still, the 55 years of family control had seen a vast transformation of the Gardens since the death of old John, and a firm base had been established on which the new company could bring prosperity. The reputation the Gardens had acquired is summed up by this reported exchange:

"'Have you ever been to Manchester?' asked a young commercial of a Worcestershire farmer. 'Manchester, na, isn't that summer Belle Vue way?'" (City Jackdaw, June 1876)

BELLE VUE (MANCHESTER) Ltd 1925-39

Initial Changes 1925-29

The new company had an authorised share capital of £200,000, made up of £150,000 in preferred ordinary shares and £50,000 in ordinary shares. The bulk of the shares and control of the company was vested in three individuals: the Chairman, Sir William Benjamin Gentle, recently retired Chief Constable of Brighton; Captain James Philip Hodge, a lawyer with financial interests, and John Henry Iles, the Managing Director. Hodge remained a "sleeping partner" and Gentle's interests were soon diverted elsewhere, so our attention falls on John Henry Iles.

Since his visit to the Gardens in 1898, Iles had become involved in the provision of fairgrounds and amusements. He laid out amusement parks in Europe and as far away as Buenos Aires, and in 1919 designed his own permanent park, the Margate Dreamland. Iles was responsible for the amusement park of the 1924 Wembley Exhibition, which was looked after by his works manager, Chris Wiseman. Iles brought Wiseman to Belle Vue to lay out the amusement park in an under-utilised area around the brewery, between the Hyde Road entrance and the athletic ground. The new amusements comprised some rides transferred from Wembley, plus a few more invented by Wiseman.

During 1925 the Flying Sea Planes, Caterpillar, Whirlpool, Whip, Jack & Jill and Hey Day were erected in the Amusement Park, while a Dodgem ride was provided next to the Monkey House. A number of profit-sharing concessionaires were brought in to operate the slot machine or amusement arcades. The rides were operated by the Company, though each ride was technically owned by its own company. Most of these were subsidiaries of Belle Vue (Manchester) Ltd, with one or two being owned by Dreamland (Margate) Ltd. The Patent Caterpillar Company was owned by J H Iles personally. The following year, after the end of the Wembley Exhibition, more rides were erected, including the River Caves, Auto Scooter, Ghost Train, Miniature Brooklands and the Scenic Railway, although some of these did not operate until 1927. The Scenic Railway was the largest attraction yet; the 1928 guide book describes it as follows:

"The Scenic Railway dominates Belle Vue. Not to see it at dark or in darkness, its cliffs picked out with lights, its vast grey body raised like a mountain range above the sports of pygmies on the plain, is to miss a thrill in anticipation. It takes you emotionally, as well as physically from the depths to the heights. It puts the wind up you, through you and round you."

Early in 1928 a miniature railway was opened, running from the Kings Hall to the Longsight entrance along The Avenue. It was operated by uniformed staff and boasted a £1,500 Barnes locomotive, purchased from a private garden line at Warburton, near Lymm. By 1934 the locomotive had been named Railway Queen, following its use at the Railway Carnivals, the popular annual event for railway employees recently introduced in the Gardens.

In many other respects, the Gardens remained unaltered, although the gasworks was closed in 1925 and its retorts used for storage. The Belle Vue band was dismissed and replaced by a jazz combo, although the military band was later reinstated.

Advertisements now appeared in the guide books, something unheard of under the old administration. The old Jennison amusements and the fireworks continued, although the battlepieces were replaced by ordinary displays without actors in 1927 and 1928. These were not a success and the old style displays resumed in 1929. The Company cut down on the production of fireworks and started to buy them from Brocks. The Lake Hotel was extended and the Hyde Road entrance altered, with new turnstiles now at the side. New company offices were created and the old pub was renamed the Hyde Road Restaurant.

The Jennisons remained in touch, for in 1926 George became involved with the erection of a long overdue memorial to the Gardens' workers who had died in the Great War. Subscriptions from employees raised over £80 and George Jennison added another £50. The memorial was erected in Gorton Cemetery and was unveiled by Angelo at a ceremony in November after a short speech by George. It contains nineteen names, including two members of the Jennison family, and still stands, now sadly defaced by vandalism.

Sir William Gentle and Greyhound Racing 1925-28

In the early 1920s an American, Charles Munn, enlisted the support of Major L Lyne Dixon, a noted coursing judge, in establishing greyhound racing in this country. Brigadier General A C Critchley and Sir William Gentle were approached over the raising of finance and in August 1925 the Greyhound Racing Association was formed. It is not known whether Gentle's interest in Belle Vue arose from any plans he had for the Gardens in this connection, but on 14th October the Association took a seven-year lease on land at the northern end of Kirkmanshulme Lane (the old brickfield, bought in 1872), at an annual rent of £276.

The choice of the North West to stage the British premiere of the sport was deliberate: it was hoped that the area's coursing tradition would aid the new form of entertainment. With a capital of £22,000, of which £8,000 was borrowed, a stadium was built on the land, and on 27th July 1926 a white-coated bugler, a striking miner from Newton Heath named Johnny Jones, opened the first meeting. Six races were run, with eight dogs in each, all of which were bought by the Association as the expected support from the area's coursing connections did not materialise.

The attendance at the first meeting was disappointing; only

John Henry Iles, Company Chairman 1928-1937

a tenth of the estimated audience of 20,000 turned up, followed by 1,600 at the next meeting. The third attracted 4,000 and by the end of the first season in October, thirty-seven meetings had been held, with an average attendance of 11,000.

The Greyhound Stadium and Belle Vue developed in partnership until Sir William Gentle became the first Chairman of the Greyhound Racing Association. He relinquished his seat on the Board of Belle Vue in 1928, and when he died in 1948 he was said to have been a rich man, although he never owned a greyhound and had never placed a single bet.

John Henry Iles and Developments 1928-33

Having achieved overall control, J H Iles was free to implement his own ideas for the Gardens. In 1929 new amusements were introduced, including the Bug and the Whirlwind Racer. A children's amusement park was laid out behind the Kings Hall, with see-saws, overboats, roundabouts and donkey rides. The most important addition was a second scenic railway, on the site of some stables next to the Hyde Road entrance, in 1929/30. Known as the Bobs, because of the shilling charge made for rides, it was purchased from a Mr Church of Buffalo, USA, for around £20,000. Its ten-car trains reached a height of 80ft by means of a 150hp motor, and fell down angles of 45°, travelling at over a mile a minute.

1928 advertisement for the Greyhound Racing Stadium

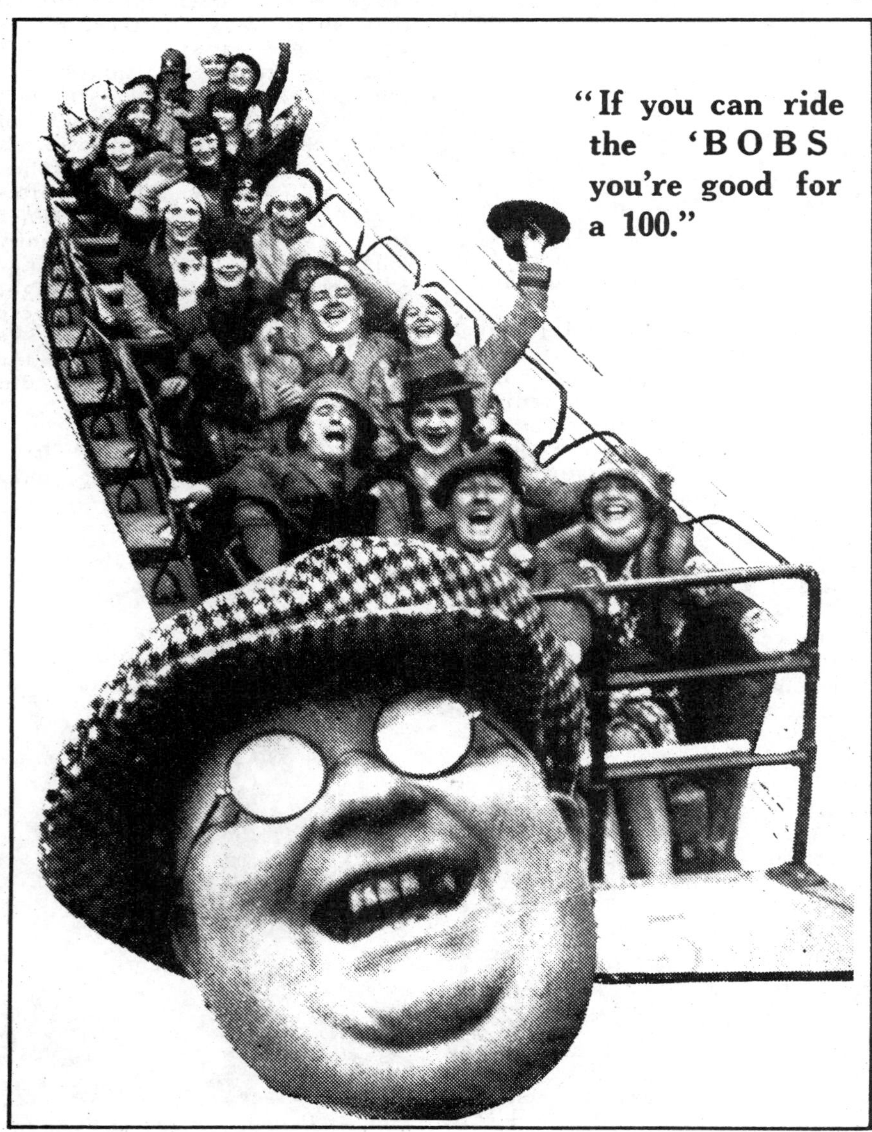

1930s advertisement for the Bobs

The old Jennison amusements were gradually removed, the Velocipedes being sold in 1931 and the Ocean Wave going shortly afterwards. The Dodgems and Over the Falls were moved from the zoo area to more appropriate locations in the Amusement Park.

The Jennison brewery ceased production in 1928. The Garibaldi Inn was sold to Allsopp's Brewery that year, and the Midland Hotel to the Openshaw Brewery Company three years later. John Jennison resigned as electrical manager in 1928, the electrical installation closed and supplies were taken from the Corporation. A series of petrol-driven generators was retained to produce electricity for the Amusement Park at peak periods. The old electrical installation building was converted to a fish restaurant. The activities of the bakery were scaled down and the printing office had closed

Getting the locomotive "Railway Queen" ready for Easter 1933

by 1931. Many of the old employees lost their jobs in these alterations, and many of the old privileges were withdrawn from the remainder.

One of the most significant innovations was the introduction of Speedway, then known as Dirt Track Racing. It was rapidly established in the recently erected greyhound racing stadium, and on 28th July 1928 a meeting was organised by International Speedways Ltd, controlled by the man who was later to own London's Windmill Theatre, Vivian van Damm. The new sport was launched at a meeting in which many star riders, some from Australia, featured. By September, the organisation of the meetings was in the hands of the North Manchester Motor Club, controlled by E O Spence, a renowned Speedway manager from London.

With the departure of Sir William Gentle and the increased separation of the affairs of the Greyhound Stadium from Belle Vue that resulted, it was decided that the sport could be better promoted in its own stadium. Late in 1928, Iles acquired a controlling interest in the North Manchester Motor Club and the Company entered into an agreement with the Club to provide Dirt Track Racing over a period of five years at a new stadium on the site of the Athletic Ground, with Spence remaining as manager. "E O", as he became known at Belle Vue, soon established a name for himself all over the North in his extensive control of speedway stadia, to the extent that the press nicknamed him the Mussolini of the North.

The new stadium opened on 23rd March 1929 and it was an immediate success. It was the largest purpose-built speedway stadium of the time. The home team, soon to be called the Aces, ran up a series of successes and individuals such as Eric Langton and Frank ("Red Devil") Varey made well deserved names for themselves. Accommodation for a further 12,000 people was provided in 1930 and the flag starting of races was replaced by an electric system devised by Spence.

The stadium was not just designed for speedway. A football pitch was laid out on the grass island in the centre and another Iles-initiated organisation, the Manchester Central Amateur Football Club, played on Sundays. This met with mixed success and was replaced by Broughton Rangers Football Club in 1933. The facilities of the former Athletic Ground were transferred to the former deer paddock between the old firework factory and the Redgate Lane end of the Gardens, where a sports ground was laid out with a wooden stand capable of seating 2,000.

Other uses of the stadium were proposed, and a series of Tattoos was held from 1928 to 1932. These were poorly attended at first, but by 1931 were successful, with an attendance that year of 85,000 over six nights. At a total cost of £10,000, and with 2,000 performers, the prices (from 1/- to 3/6d) were claimed to be the "lowest for which a Tattoo of this nature has been offered". Encouraged by this, a five year "Pageant Plan" was announced, the first being the Lancashire Cotton Pageant of 1932. The scenario for this was devised by Matthew Anderson and the producer was Edward P Genn, who had been responsible for the Pageant of Transport at Liverpool, part of the Liverpool & Manchester Railway Centenary Celebrations in 1930.

Held in the Stadium, the Cotton Pageant was divided into twelve episodes:
1 Persian Market Scene
2 The Court of King William the Conqueror
3 Lancashire Witches
4 A Cotton Plantation
5 The Age of Invention
6 The Revolt against the Machines
7 The Progress of Transport

Trophy winners of the 1931 Speedway season: Walter Hull, Max Grosskreutz, Chun Moore, Arthur Franklyn, Larry Boulton, Eric Langton, Bob Harrison and Frank Varey

8 The Massacre of Peterloo
9 Lancashire Market Day
10 Lancashire at Work
11 Lancashire at Play
12 Lancashire Cotton for the World

The final episode was described as *"the biggest and most impressive finale ever devised. King Cotton enters the arena in a large triumphal car, dragged by 800 children, led by 1,000 mannequins dressed in Lancashire fabrics, people of all nations troop into the arena, followed by characteristic vehicles from every part of the world. 12,000 people pay homage to King Cotton and raise their voices in the Cotton Pageant Anthem 'The Red Rose'. This, the most magnificent Pageant ever performed, closes with Sir Hubert Parry's glorious hymn 'Jerusalem'. The Lancashire Cotton Pageant will live in your memory as the finest spectacle of the century."*

An artistic triumph the Pageant undoubtedly was, but its value to the ailing cotton industry was doubtful, and for Belle Vue it was not a financial success as only 200,000 people were attracted, 50,000 fewer than forecast. The Five Year Plan was quietly dropped.

The Kings Hall also saw many new activities. It ceased to have the appearance of a wooden barn when arena-type seating for 6,000 was installed around a central stage, at a cost of £30,000. In 1928 it was the venue for the Railway Carnival and the crowning of the Railway Queen, who symbolised goodwill between railwaymen at home and abroad.

A series of boxing contests was initiated in 1929, followed by wrestling in 1930. Celebrity concerts were tried, without much success at first and with even less later, when the admission prices were reduced and the public felt that the concerts had acquired a cheap image.

The most important use to which the Kings Hall was put, and for which it had been primarily adapted, was the annual Christmas Circus. This event was staged through the assistance of Tom Bickerstaffe, Chairman of Blackpool Tower Company, who had been brought on to the Board when J H Iles gained overall control in 1928. A summer circus had been operating at Blackpool for many years and it was decided to duplicate this at Belle Vue each Christmas.

The first circus was held over the winter of 1929/30, with the Blackpool ringmaster, George Lockhart, in charge. Fred Bonelli, who had made his debut at Belle Vue in 1928, was responsible for the music. The circus was an immediate success and a summer circus followed in July and August, this time without Lockhart. This was a failure and was not repeated, but the Christmas Circus and Lockhart himself soon established a reputation for Belle Vue which lasted for decades.

The programme for the 1930/31 circus contained sixteen star acts, including Doodles the Clown, the Ten Asgards (springboard act), Powers' Dancing Elephants, the Graceful Zerba Sisters (Caucasian Equestriennes), Les Wassilians (Oriental Pas de Deux), V Truibka with a mixed troupe of lions, polar bears and dogs, Madel Regal's unrideable mules and many other acts from this country and abroad. The circus was held twice daily from 22nd December to the end of January. George Lockhart was billed as the Prince of Ringmasters.

Musical Contests 1925-39

John Henry Iles's involvement with Belle Vue was greeted with relief in the brass band world, which was apprehensive over the future of the contests, since 1900 known as the British Open Brass Band Championships. Iles took an immediate interest, arranging for new and original test pieces to be composed for the event. The first was the tone poem "Macbeth" by Dr Thomas Keighley, Professor of Organ and Composition at the Royal Manchester College of Music. Keighley provided other pieces of a Shakespearian nature in subsequent years. Iles conducted the massed band concert that followed the September contest until his death in 1951. Despite his close affinity with the brass band movement, he was not highly regarded as a conductor, being

Princess Mary inspecting Girl Guides in the newly-opened Speedway Stadium, June 1929

said to have rather a wooden technique.

The hand bell ringing competitions ended in 1926 and the choral and concertina contests the following year. A series of bugle band competitions started in 1928.

A restructuring of the May and July brass band contests took place in 1931, and in 1933 the National Brass Band Competition Rules were introduced. In the February of the same year, contests for Mission and Social Institute Bands were started. In 1934, entrants to the July competition were expected to take part in a marching contest. To celebrate the King's Silver Jubilee in 1935, a "monster band demonstration" was held in the Stadium, the patriotic march "England" being conducted by Iles. A massed concert, involving some 2,700 performers, was held the following year in the same venue; this time the conducting was shared by Iles and the ever versatile Fred Bonelli.

The Mission and Social Institute Band Contests were not a success and had been discontinued by 1938. The military band and bugle band contests, which had been established in 1900 and 1928 respectively, also did not fare so well and took place for the last time in 1939, casualties of the Second World War.

Company Affairs and Exhibitions 1929-36

The substantial investment by the new Company between the years 1925 and 1929 was achieved at the expense of the shareholders. In fact, no ordinary share dividend was paid until after the Second World War. George Jennison, sitting on the sidelines, thought that the Company had invested too rapidly for its own good, and he predicted bankruptcy and the quick demise of Speedway. But neither of these was to be.

The potential of the Exhibition Hall was high on the list of priorities and in 1930 it underwent refurbishment and a 12,000 sq ft Exhibition Hall Cafe was provided. At the same time the Hot Water Room, to the rear of the Kings Hall, was moved into the Exhibition Hall building. The Hall itself totalled some 61,000 sq ft and was said to be the largest in the North of England. It still possessed two railway sidings for use by exhibitors, but these were rarely used.

The mortgages to the Jennison family had been slightly reduced in 1929, whilst in July that year a set of third mortgage debentures in the sum of £25,000 was issued to Lloyds Bank City Office Nominees Ltd. Two years later the working capital of the Company was increased by a further £100,000 through the issue of £75,000 worth of cumulative preference shares and another £25,000 in preferred ordinary shares. In December, payment on the original preference shares was some six months in arrears and the Company had acquired a reputation for being tardy in settling accounts.

It is not difficult to see why these problems had arisen. The enormous capital expenditure had produced new facilities to widen the attraction of the Gardens, but in order to produce the necessary profits, these had to be put to regular and intensive use. Some innovations, like the circus, wrestling and speedway, were successful, and others, like the Broughton Rangers venture, were not. If the Gardens were to recover from their long term decline, there was no option but to pursue this policy and to diversify and expand the activities. It is said that on occasions Iles dipped his hand into his own pocket to keep the Company solvent and no doubt there is some truth in this. The relative failure of the Cotton Pageant must have been a big disappointment. Still, there were signs that things were moving in the right direction and profits for the year ending October 1932 were £13,077, up £8,038 on the previous year.

Strenuous efforts were made to publicise the attractions of the Gardens and the Exhibition Hall to the organisers of rallies, political gatherings and exhibitions. The "Belle Vue News Sheet" was started. Early editions advertised the introduction of new speedboats, motor launches and pedal boats on the lakes, and the numerous catering establishments, said to seat 8,640 in total. Charabancs could be parked free of charge, either in the large parking area between Redgate Lane and Longsight Station, or on the six other "huge parking grounds".

The catering establishments included the Imperial, Japanese, First, Princess, Emperor and Gallery tea rooms; the Chinese, First Class and Oriental cafes; the Hyde Road and Fish restaurants; the Club Room, the Exhibition Hall Restaurant and Hot Water Room. Events in the Exhibition Hall in 1932 included the Northern Counties Terrier Show, the Manchester Championship Dog Show, the Grocers' Exhibition, Manchester Pigeon Show and the Textile Recorder Machinery Exhibition. The Ford

A competitor and its owner at the Belle Vue Bulldog Show, September 1930

Motor Company held a motor show in the Ballroom. The Gardens were visited by HRH Prince George in 1932, the first official royal visit.

1933 saw a major refurbishment of the Ballroom, into which were introduced "novel lighting effects". The Amusement Park was improved by the laying of 28,400 sq yds of asphalt and the laying out of twelve large flower beds. The Speedway arena was refurbished. In August, the last financial links with the Jennison family were severed when the first and second mortgage debentures were redeemed and a new mortgage entered into for £150,000 with the Legal & General Insurance Co. Together with the earlier mortgage to Lloyds Bank, the Company's indebtedness amounted to £175,000. The alterations in the Company's financing meant a saving of £1,000 a year in interest charges. Iles's son, H F B Iles (often referred to as "Mr Eric") became a director in 1933. Tom Bickerstaffe died in February 1934, creating a vacancy on the Board.

1934 events included a large Youth Rally in celebration of a royal visit to Manchester, which ended with a firework display showing the royal portraits. The Manchester Flower Show was held in July and the severe drought of that year was overcome by drawing water from one of the old wells, disused for several years. Sir Oswald Mosley appeared at a Fascist demonstration in September, and further controversy was caused when a theatrical garden party, organised for a Sunday to allow actors (including the young Anna Neagle) to attend, was postponed to a Wednesday following the intervention of the Lord's Day Observance Society. Events in the Kings Hall were gauged by a "Mirthometer", a device invented by the Company's electrical engineer, J Edgar, and consisting of four microphones and a recording chart, which measured the amount of laughter and applause.

A great Temperance Rally attracted 90,000 visitors in 1935. In November, Belle Vue featured in a film, "Animal Pie", made by the Manchester Film Society assisted by the American star, Buddy Rogers.

Profits for 1934 sank to £4,581, recovering to £7,831 in 1935. No interest was paid on the preferred ordinary shares from 1934 and unrest among the smaller shareholders would shortly begin. However, there was considerable optimism about a big effort to be made for Centenary Year, 1936.

Broughton Rangers and other Sports

With the failure of Manchester Central AFC, J H Iles sought other uses for the Stadium, which, apart from special occasions, was used only two evenings a week for speedway meetings. The opportunity came in 1933, when the long established Broughton Rangers Rugby League Football Club, which played at the Cliff, Higher Broughton, was in financial difficulties. Iles arranged for a new company to be formed, with George Wilson and himself on the Board, and Belle Vue invested £4,000 in the venture. A 21-year lease for the use of the Belle Vue Stadium on certain nights of the week was drawn up, the rental being based on attendances.

George Wilson, General Manager of the Belle Vue Company from 1925 to 1941

The club's first year at the Gardens was not a success and in April 1934 all the original directors resigned by mutual agreement. Five were later reappointed to a smaller Board. Moderate successes were being achieved by the end of 1935, but heavy financial losses were incurred during the first three years and these had to be underwritten by the Belle Vue Company, which attracted the wrath of some shareholders. Following the announcement of a loss of £2,828, rumours that the Club was being transferred back to the Cliff were quickly denied. The recruitment of expensive players was cut back in favour of the long term cultivation of juniors.

In August 1937, to restore flagging attendances, it was announced that, in line with the practice at speedway meetings, season tickets for the Club and the Gardens would be interchangeable. Although attendances continued to be disappointing, this did have some effect as the 1937 loss was reduced to £1,935 and the 1938 loss to £1,002.

Other new sports were tried out in the Stadium. 1931 had seen chariot racing, and although a crowd of 25,000 was attracted, the experiment was not repeated. In May 1934 Midget Car Racing was introduced. The cars did not possess brakes and the sport was described as a forerunner of Stock Car

Railway Queen Patricia Clark and Circus ponies, January 1932

Racing. The crowds were not thrilled by the new sport and it was soon relegated to occupying slots in mixed programmes at Speedway events. After a few years it was discontinued completely.

In March 1935 another attempt was made to establish a new sport with the setting up of a baseball team, the Belle Vue Tigers. Its success was short lived and matches continued only until 1936.

Throughout the 1930s the Kings Hall was virtually the Boxing Mecca of Europe - British, European, Empire and World title fights were held there, featuring local champions. The first World Championship bout took place on 30th October 1932, when Jackie Brown of Manchester, British flyweight champion, beat the Tunisian Young Perez. The following July saw bantamweight Johnny King challenge world champion Al Brown of Panama. King lost narrowly on points. Another name notable at this time was Jock McAvoy, the "Rochdale Thunderbolt", British and Empire middleweight champion for twelve years and outright winner of a Lonsdale Belt.

Wrestling, too, featured prominently, especially during the later 1930s when promotion of the sport at Belle Vue was undertaken by Kathleen Look, the country's only woman promoter. She married E O Spence and was followed in the later 1940s by a husband and wife team, Jessie and Dick Rogers, the latter refereeing the matches.

Zoological Developments 1925-35

Throughout 1925 George Jennison was general adviser and zoological superintendent to the Company and all his suggestions were carried out. In August 1925 he again arranged with the BBC to make an outside broadcast at the Zoo. This time the commentator was Victor Smythe and Jennison records, "not one of the animals failed us, and some extras obliged so that we more than fulfilled our contract to the BBC". At the end of his duties, George Jennison valued the zoological collection at £6,893-15s.

1925 saw the death of the only woman keeper, Mrs Lambert, aged 52. First appointed in 1916 on the death of her husband, also a keeper, Mrs Lambert was described by George Jennison as having "a strange power of control over most of her animals". The tigress, Stella, was the exception and the tragedy took place on 8th November when Mrs Lambert was cleaning out the tigress's cage. She had failed to ensure that Stella was locked securely in her sleeping compartment and called out to her assistant, her nephew Edgar Worthington, for help. When he arrived he saw his aunt lying in the entrance to the sleeping compartment and was unable to force the tigress back. Senior keeper James Craythorne arrived with a gun, but it was too late. Mrs Lambert was buried in Gorton Cemetery, her coffin being carried by six keepers, and the Gardens were closed to the public that day. Her tombstone remains to this day, bearing a painting of the tigress's head.

George Jennison in 1933. In his later years he was active in politics for the Liberal Party. After he relinquished control of Belle Vue in 1925, he published several books, including "Noah's Cargo", but his great manuscript on Belle Vue was never published

When J H Iles took over in 1928 he put his brother, William Butler Iles, in charge of the Zoo, the catering department and the Brass Band contests. W B Iles was also a director and he had been involved with theatre and show business, at one time managing the Lyceum Theatre, Taunton. The following year improvements were put in hand in the Zoo. A new Reptile House was opened adjacent to the Orange and Camellia House, which had been gradually assuming the role of a reptile house since before the Great War. Most of the live specimens were now transferred from the Museum to more suitable accommodation. In the same year, the latest Jennison amusement, Over the Falls, was moved from its position adjacent to the Paddock House, and replaced by the Rocky Mountain Enclosure, an artificial rockwork structure for mountain species designed by Chris Wiseman and based on the ideas of German zoologist Carl Hagenbeck. The fame of the latter's Hamburg Zoo, with its bar-less enclosures and near natural animal habitat, was becoming widespread. The new enclosure was inhabited by Corsican moufflon and Barbary sheep. No other zoological improvements were carried out

Keepers and a young female Indian elephant, with a side view of part of the firework picture

until 1930, when the Penguin House was converted to an aquarium, the tank being filled with various types of freshwater fish. This innovation was not successful and was discontinued in 1933, when the building was restocked with penguins.

To relieve the burden on his brother's shoulders, J H Iles engaged George Jennison as zoological adviser, at a salary of 100 guineas per annum from May 1932. The former managing director had been a freelance consultant since 1926, although it is suspected that he did not find much call for his services. His responsibilities at Belle Vue were to inspect the animals four times a year.

Jennison found the value of the collection had declined since 1926 as a result of neglect and lack of specialist attention. Many of the cages contained rabbits, common cockatoos and other cheap animals, and some were empty. Little attempt was made to exercise the animals that could be exercised, and rats, so often a problem in zoos, were present in large numbers. He found a new enclosure for kangaroos too damp. Jennison's quarterly reports contained many recommendations but few were carried out.

This state of affairs was not to last, for in March 1933 W B Iles retired and the Zoo was provided with a full-time superintendent, his son, Gerald, aged 21. Gerald had come to the Gardens in 1928 with his father and had first worked in the Time Office before taking a course in Zoology at Manchester University in 1930. At the time of his appointment, he was the youngest person to have been offered such a responsible post and he rapidly established reputations for himself and for the Zoo.

The young Iles assembled a library of useful books and attended to the labelling of each cage or enclosure, taking care to illustrate the large name plates with maps showing the species' origin or geographical distribution. One of his earliest decisions was to close the old Natural History Museum, which contained mainly stuffed birds of considerable age and past their best in appearance. He proposed to use the space for an aquarium, a feature absent since the short-lived experiment in the Penguin House. Iles thought that a separate admission charge would enable the display to pay its way, but soon found out that his family ties were not enough to secure approval for his plans. The Board turned the idea down, saying that the space was needed for other purposes. The Museum remained closed, though intact, and proposals were made to reopen it at various times up to 1937. Its contents were finally dispersed in 1941, when the skeleton of Maharajah and some other exhibits were acquired by the Manchester Museum, where the skeleton is still displayed.

As well as providing the professionalism and dedication necessary to run the Zoo, Iles was a good publicist and soon realised that many of his proposals would only stand a chance of coming to fruition if attendances were satisfactory. He is mentioned in the local press as early as June 1933 and for the next twenty years the newspapers were never short of stories from Belle Vue, often concerning new animals. Iles used animals, especially snakes, in talks given to parties of children and others at theatres, church halls, etc.

Bernard A Hastain, scenic artist 1912-33. He came to Belle Vue as assistant to R Caney

Despite the problems encountered with his uncle over the financing of new projects, Gerald Iles was able to effect a number of changes in his first year of office. On the banks of the Picture Lake, where Laughter Land had been, an outdoor enclosure for pumas called the South Terrace was erected. An enclosure for deer was provided adjacent to the Maze Cottage and the Kirkmanshulme Lane boundary wall. This was described as the Deer Park, which name was also given to a smaller enclosure close to the Tree Island Pond. Deer also replaced ostriches in Danson's Asiatic Kiosk, now named the Octagon. Iles also announced plans for a new lion house, an insect house, a new museum, an aquarium and a rebuilding of the reptile house to take Nile crocodiles. With the exception of the aquarium, none of these schemes came to fruition.

The Zoo encountered bad publicity in June 1934 when, at the instigation of the RSPCA, James Craythorne and some keepers rounded up two wild swans and their family of nine cygnets at a pool in Denton. A crowd of some 200 local people demonstrated against the capture and the police had to be called in. The swans settled quite happily at Belle Vue, where they were

Giraffe enclosure with Giraffe, Camel and Rhino House in the background

free from the interference they suffered at their former home.

Towards the end of 1934 two more relics of the Jennison era were removed. The Maze and the Figure Eight Toboggan were replaced by a new sunken garden at a cost of £5,000. Members of the Broughton Rangers team assisted in laying this out, and it was opened by the wife of bandleader Jack Hylton. Also displaced by this alteration were the old hexagonal enclosures for wolves and foxes; the animals were given new accommodation between the Tree Island Pond and the Sports Ground.

In 1935 Gerald Iles carried out improvements to the Elephant House. Each stall was enlarged and the old iron and oak posts which had kept the animals in were replaced by short spikes and a moat. The accommodation for the hippo was enlarged and given a new heated pool, with access to an outdoor yard and pool. At the same time, the profusion of smaller cages was removed from inside the building. Also in 1935, a modest aquarium was set up, consisting of four tanks in a corner of the Reptile House. Unfortunately all the fish died when the water overheated owing to a faulty or deliberately altered thermostat, but the popularity of the attraction led to the stock being quickly replaced and plans were advanced for a larger aquarium to be opened the following year.

Firework Displays 1930-39

Following the resumption of the old battlepiece displays in 1929, it became apparent that the format was dated and that greater sophistication was demanded by audiences now accustomed to the "Talkies". The 1933 display, "The Massacre of Cawnpore", was therefore provided with a running commentary, read by Bernard Hastain. It also featured one of the elephants, Nellie, and a large waterfall, 100ft high and 50ft wide. Hastain died of war wounds in November that year and, as a mark of respect, his last spectacle was repeated the following year. George Jennison remarks that although Hastain was not a particularly good artist, he had a better sense of theatrical effect than his predecessors.

No scenic artist was appointed until 1935, when Owen Simpson took over. The display that year was entitled "Sudan, the Destiny of Egypt". The display of 1936, "San Sebastian 1836", was the first in which girls took part. The cast of 250 included 20 Belle Vue Belles, dressed in colourful Spanish costumes, in a ballet sequence. Acrobats and cycling elephants also appeared, and special "parachute rockets" were supplied by Brocks, on to which searchlights were played with great effect. Music for the ballet scenes was composed, arranged and selected by Bonelli.

The 1937 display, "The Golden Pagoda of Rangoon", was marred when one of the extras, Edward Caffrey, aged 57, was crushed to death by one of the two-ton scenery trucks as he stopped to change costume. The inquest recorded a verdict of "accidental death".

The following year's show saw a change of style, when "Fantasy Battle" was based on a fairy story theme. 1939 saw a return to the traditional style, with "India 1757". The season's show was cut short at the end of August by the outbreak of the Second World War.

Despite the changes in style of the displays, the continued success of Belle Vue in this field must be partly credited to the efficient way in which the army of actors was organised. Since the Great War these had been mainly ex-servicemen, drilled and trained by Sergeant Bramwell, formerly of the King's Own Regiment. Also noteworthy is the effort that went into the preparation and burning of a huge effigy of Guy Fawkes every 5th November. This took several weeks to build, wore a size 25 hat and reached a height of 20ft in the sitting position. In 1936 the Guy was burnt on the Paddock sports ground with the aid of 80 tons of material, including 25 pianos, 24 barrels of oil and 1 cwt of pitch. Visitors to the 1930s displays recall vividly the huge exodus of rats from around the stage and scenery when the shows began, and also the mass consumption of "Tattis" potato crisps, a necessary adjunct to one's enjoyment of the displays.

Belle Vue's Guy Fawkes, a monster effigy, the burning of which was an annual feature from the 1930s to the 1950s

The Centenary Celebrations 1936

In a bid to break away from the dismal profit levels encountered in the early 1930s, a major effort was put into the 1936 celebration commemorating the centenary of the Gardens. It was also the opportunity for Gerald Iles to implement some of his ideas.

Preparatory work started in November 1935, when the old bakery, gasworks and printing office were cleared, the elephant Nellie assisting in the demolition. In January, plans for the new Centenary Gardens at the Hyde Road entrance were announced and work began. The entire project would cost about £50,000. The first part to be finished was a two-sided, electrically operated clock, surmounted by a statue of Buddha, near the entrance. The clock bore animal designs on one side and a representation of speedway trophies or riders on the other. The floral displays were to be changed annually.

The Centenary Gardens were completed by Easter and contained a large gibbon cage, 40ft square and 25ft high. This had its own central house for the animals which was electrically lit, heated and equipped with "Vita" glass sun verandahs. The temperature of the house was thermostatically controlled and the building made draught proof, being insulated with fibreglass packed tightly between the inner and outer walls. Special windscreens were placed round each corner of the outer walls so that the inmates could shelter from cold winds. Twenty Hoolock gibbons were introduced to the cage in May. To cater for their natural instincts, their new cage was equipped with ropes, swings, a tightrope and a bathing pool.

Beyond the Gibbon Cage, a Monkey Mountain was formed, consisting of a central pile of artificial rock surrounded by a water-filled trench, the whole structure lacking bars of any description. On one side, water tumbled down a series of cascades into a pool which overflowed into the trench, whilst high up was a heated space inside the rock which served as sleeping accommodation. 100 rhesus monkeys were the first tenants. Next to them was a Raccoon Pit, also uncaged, for six of the animals. It had its own tree, pool, waterfall and half-timbered Elizabethan house. Surrounding the Centenary Gardens area was a sea of 20,000 tulips and a similar number of wallflowers, whilst the floral clock also had forget-me-nots and polyanthus.

Other improvements that year included an ornamental rock garden for alpine plants in an old pool near the Paddock Range. This was used as an open-air reptilium and stocked with 100 English vipers from the New Forest, together with other hardy snakes and lizards. An open-air lion cub villa was provided on the South Terrace, and new cages provided for parrots, pheasants and cranes. A penguin pool and rhino enclosure were proposed, and the latter was later built next to the Camel House when an infant rhino, Faro, was bought. It was the first in the Zoo's collection for twenty years; unfortunately the animal died shortly after arrival.

Though the Centenary Gardens were a success in appearance, in practice they had noticeable drawbacks. The placing of the house in the centre of the Gibbon Cage was a mistake, as the animals had a habit of attacking keepers, especially when the one that was being sought found refuge in the house. This shortcoming was rectified 21 years later, when the cage was removed to another part of the Gardens. The gibbons did not survive very long in the cage, for by 1938 only three of the original complement remained.

The Raccoon Pit had to be substantially repaired within two years when it was found that the normally gentle animals had been systematically removing the tiles of the surrounds at night. Further problems, connected with the contamination of the water in the pool, caused the raccoons to be replaced by coypus later. The Monkey Mountain was more successful, several instances of breeding occurring in its early years. The water-filled moat was not wide enough to stop monkeys escaping on several occasions, especially in winter when the water froze. This tendency was partly cured when, within sight of the rest of the colony, two escapees were captured, consigned to a box and taken to secure houses elsewhere.

Two tigons, Kliou and Maude, arrived on 24th July 1936, having been brought from Dresden Zoo by Hagenbeck of Hamburg. Gerald Iles had been trying to secure these hybrid animals, born of a Manchurian tiger and African lioness, since 1932. The novel appearance of the tigons was an immediate success, although brother and sister did not get on well with each other and soon had to be separated.

Other parts of the Gardens saw improvements for the centenary celebrations. The miniature railway was doubled in length by the construction of a loop at the Longsight end which passed through a tunnel in the Nursery Gardens and over three level crossings. "Parkside Station", next to the Kings Hall, was provided with a traverser and double track layout, enabling locomotives to run round the trains. The engine shed was extended to accommodate new

View of the Centenary Gardens, showing the floral clock, Gibbon Cage and Bobs

rolling stock and an additional locomotive and five covered carriages were obtained from Southend. The locomotive, "George the Fifth", manufactured by Bassett Lowke in 1911, proved to be underpowered for the work it was required to do at Belle Vue, and it was relegated to lighter duties. The old Roller Skating Rink in the Ballroom block was converted into the Tudor Restaurant.

The Centenary Gardens were formally opened by the Lord Mayor of Manchester, Alderman T S Williams, on 8th April. He was flanked by a guard of honour of 24 of Sergeant Bramwell's extras dressed in red tunics of 1836. The admission proceeds went to the Manchester & Salford Medical Charities Fund and the Lord Mayor's Unemployment Relief Fund. Easter that year was cold, but the investments had proved attractive and there was a record attendance.

Gerald Iles's aquarium plans were finally realised on 1st May when a new display was opened in an extension of the Reptile House by Gracie Fields. Containing some 400 fish in 20 tanks, heated by hot water pipes at a temperature of 75°F, it had only just been completed in time.

Scenes from the Rock Studios film "Cotton Queen", starring Stanley Holloway and Mary Lawson and directed by Bernard Vorhaus, were shot in the Gardens during July. The studios had been started two years earlier by John Henry Iles and and American, Joe Rock, in an attempt to establish a British counterpart to the American-dominated film industry. Rock was confident that "Cotton Queen" would be "one of the most outstanding British films ever produced", but today it is hard to find any mention of it in the standard film reference books.

A large Conservative Party rally was held in July and attended by Neville Chamberlain.

The firework display for that evening included a large picture of his father. In the same month, a Zoo Shop was opened, another of Gerald Iles's ideas. This sold all sizes of live specimens, but one imagines that orders for the larger species were rather infrequent!

The improvements carried out in 1936 had proved their worth, for in the year up to October net profits were more than doubled to £16,210. But with such a highly geared enterprise as Belle Vue, several years of prosperity would have to succeed one another before arrears of interest on the cumulative and preferred ordinary shares could be paid off to allow payment of dividend to the ordinary shareholders. The payment of the directors' full remuneration for the first time did not endear itself to the disgruntled minor shareholders, many of whom were beginning to get agitated at the lack of return on their investment.

The Prelude to War 1937-39

Following the success of the 1936 season, the Company sought to capitalise on the coronation of George VI in 1937. £10,000 was spent on the ballroom, which was redecorated and given a new dance floor, 160ft by 100ft, of New Zealand mati wood. The bandstand area was removed from the balcony and placed on the dance floor and a new heating system was installed. It was officially named the Coronation Ballroom and featured, for the first time, Old Tyme Dance sessions organised by Bonelli.

The ice spectacular "Marina" was held in May in the Kings Hall, using a temporary rink 50 to 60ft in diameter. The ice-making plant was kept for future shows. A total of 98 artistes appeared, including some from Russia, America and Hungary. The show was a success and was repeated in 1938 as "Ice Time". In July 1939 "Ice Scream" was put on

The fourth generation of Craythornes, keepers of snakes and small mammals, photographed in 1933. He is holding a kusimanse

by impresario Claude Langdon. This "crazy show on skates" incorporated comedy, ballet and acrobatic scenes, as well as a game of badminton played on ice. Another success of 1937 was the first Manchester Evening News Ideal Home Exhibition, which attracted over 50,000 visitors in its first seven days.

A number of zoological improvements were undertaken in 1937. A new rhino enclosure was formed, using blocks of stone 3½ft long from the old City Gaol building to protect the trees. After the death of Freddie, the last orang-utan, work started on converting the Ape House into a Cubs Nursery, another of Gerald Iles's proposals. This was provided with a teak floor and was used for breeding and showing young animals. On its eastern side, several old refreshment buildings were removed to form an outdoor paddock with pool. Gerald Iles was particularly fond of lions and tigers, and the offspring of the big cats were to be the

Advertisement for the 1936 firework display

most frequent occupants of the building.

At the end of the year proposals were made to move another favourite feature of the zoo, the Happy Family, from the old Bird of Prey Terrace adjoining the Camel House to a new cage next to the Sealion House. Started in the later Jennison era by keeper James Craythorne, Happy Family was an attempt to show that animals, if brought up together, will respect each other. Thus, at one time the cage, with its miniature house, "Happiholme", contained guinea pigs, doves, bantams and cats. The proposed move did not take place. Another unusual enclosure of the time was the Outcast Paddock, where the losers of fights and squabbles with mates were placed. Here, widely differing species seemingly enjoyed a peaceful co-existence.

A red fox, Sammy, escaped in 1937; he evaded capture and caused trouble for six years. In October, the first giraffe was born at the zoo. Named Pax, the animal received much publicity through the efforts of Gerald Iles. Unfortunately, Pax did not live long and it was two years before another giraffe, Doreen, was born. She produced her own offspring in the 1950s.

The years 1934 to 1937 saw considerable rationalisation of Belle Vue's land holdings. The leases on the land between Stockport Road and Longsight Station were allowed to lapse and a large area adjacent to Pink Bank Lane was sold to the Corporation, who built the Belle Vue housing estate there. Other plots were sold to the Council over the years, particularly on the north side of Belle Vue Street, where a school and ambulance station were erected, and on Kirkmanshulme Lane, where a school and the Greenwood House flats were built.

These disposals by the Company released capital for improvements and kept up profit levels. However, in 1937 it was necessary to arrange a further loan of £25,000 from the Westminster Bank. In 1937 the Greyhound Stadium was sold to the Greyhound Racing Association for £70,000. In order to protect the Company's interests, the Association was required not to use the stadium for anything other than greyhound racing, and not to sell alcohol except within a licensed club.

The profits for the year ending October 1937 had increased to £17,500, but the Annual General Meeting the following April was dominated by another matter. John Henry Iles had quietly resigned his positions as Chairman and Managing Director in 1937 in anticipation of his bankruptcy. His venture into the film industry had lost him his personal fortune, reputedly in the region of £250,000. Much of his work at Belle Vue was taken over by his son, and by the Chief Administrator, George Wilson, who became the Managing Director. In due course Rock Studios were wound up and Iles was declared bankrupt.

The Company's attitude towards Iles was generous, reflecting his commitment to the Company in its early days and the continued involvement of his family in its management. Debts of £17,500 which he owed the Company were written off pending realisation of his estate, and he was paid £5,000 for special services in connection with the sale of the Greyhound Stadium. He remained as a technical adviser, although his involvement with Belle Vue from now on was limited to his first love, the Brass Band concerts. The 1938 Annual General Meeting was a surprisingly subdued affair, but a request for George Jennison to be elected as a director was not carried. From this time H F B Iles was the dominant personality in running the Company, and 1938 saw "Eric" expressing concern about the capacity of the bars in the stadium, where he thought profits could be improved. George Jennison died suddenly on 21st October 1938.

Gerald Iles continued to make modest improvements to the Zoo. In March 1938 the old Tree Island Pond was reconstructed in Japanese style and other cages and enclosures were renewed or enlarged. The Bear Pits were relined with green concrete blocks, provided with better methods of operating the doors to the sleeping dens and given new teak floors. Camel rides were reintroduced when a camel was acquired, filling a gap in the collection since 1936. Six to eight children could be pulled using an ingenious chariot.

In January 1939 two alligators were stolen by two former employees. The unfortunate animals died after being abandoned in the snow, but were soon replaced by animals given as gifts. In March, it was announced that a Pets Corner was planned, and in May Caesar, the first adult rhino for 22 years, arrived. Gerald Iles was also making efforts to obtain a giant panda and a sloth bear, for which a new pit would be needed. In August, improvements were made at the aquarium, which now contained 23 tanks, of which 19 held tropical fish. The central viewing passage was roofed in to prevent reflections in the glass of the brightly lit tanks

TEAS.

SPECIAL HIGH TEA.
Tea
Cold Salmon and Cucumber with Mayonnaise
Cold Roast Chicken and Ham
Green Salad
Peach Melba
Brown and White Bread and Butter
4/6

HIGH TEA.	HIGH TEA.
Tea	Tea
Brown and White Bread and Butter	White and Brown Bread and Butter
Roast Chicken and Ham	Salmon
Green Salad	Mayonnaise
Mixed Fancies	Green Salad
	Lamb and Mint Sauce
	Cake
3/3	**3/6**

STANDARD TEA.
Tea
White and Brown Bread and Butter
Ham and Tongue
Green Salad : Cream Ice
2/6

TEAS.

SPECIAL FISH TEA.	FISH TEA.
Tea	Tea
White and Brown Bread and Butter	Bread and Butter
Fried Filleted Plaice	Fried Sole
Chipped Potatoes	Chipped Potatoes
Fruit Cake	Vanilla Ice
2/6	**2/-**

FISH TEA	HAM TEA.
Tea	Tea
White or Brown Bread and Butter	Bread and Butter
Fried Fillet of Fish	Cold Ham & Tongue
Chipped Potatoes	
1/6	**1/6**

FRUIT TEA	POPULAR TEA.
Tea	Tea
Bread and Butter	Bread and Butter
Fruit Salad & Cream	Fruit and Custard
Cake	
1/6	**1/3**

Address Enquiries to—
MANAGER, CATERING DEPT. BELLE VUE, MANCHESTER 12.

From the Belle Vue "Catering for Parties" leaflet, 1938 season

and to stop the growth of algae.

Punch & Judy shows were put on between 27th May and 30th September by Professor le Fay of Quarmby Road, Gorton. His contract stipulated four performances daily, each of a different character and title, with two extra performances on specified days if required. Each show had to last at least twenty minutes, have a "clean script and well dressed puppets" and be given when and where decided by the management. For this he was paid £8 a week. The amusement rides for the 1939 season included Jack and Jill, Over the Falls, Bug, Whirlwind Racer, River Caves, Scenic Railway, Bobs, Seaplanes, Ghost Train, Skooters, Coaster Cars and the Hall of Laughter.

The Company's fortunes were now reasonably high, but still not high enough to satisfy the shareholders. The 1938 profits had slipped back to £15,022. Bad summer weather, increased unemployment and the Munich crisis were blamed. However, speedway attendances were improving and higher receipts were taken from the restyled Ballroom.

YEARS OF SUCCESS AND DECLINE 1939-56

Wartime 1939-45

The outbreak of war had been anticipated for some time. Indeed, as early as 1933 there had been two firework displays entitled "Air Raid on London". An ARP demonstration was given on Firework Island in 1938, and during 1939 the staff were trained in Civil Defence work, including fire fighting. Standpipes were erected and arrangements were made to pump water from the lakes. Windows were covered with strips of gummed paper to minimise the danger from bomb blast.

The Gardens opened as usual on Sunday 3rd September, when one of the Gorton Philharmonic Orchestra's "open rehearsals" was scheduled for 11.00am in the Kings Hall. Although a fair crowd of people had turned up, the concert did not take place because of Chamberlain's broadcast, and the Gardens closed entirely at noon. The military authorities immediately took control of parts of the Gardens, including the Exhibition Hall, many of the restaurants and the top floor of the administrative offices, except Gerald Iles's office. The sports ground became a barrage balloon base and air-raid shelters were dug. An early casualty was the Asiatic Kiosk at the Longsight entrance, then used for ostriches, which had to be emptied. Apart from this, the Zoo remained untouched and an eerie silence fell over the place.

The Manchester Emergency Committee was concerned about the potential danger of animals escaping as a result of bomb damage, and arrangements were made with George Wilson to arm the keepers with rifles and ask some of them to do duty at night. Most of the animals were not considered dangerous, but a list of those to be shot on escape was drawn up. It comprised thirteen lions, six tigers, two leopards, one cheetah, two tigons, the bears and three other small cats. Two poisonous snakes were to be left to their own devices as it was expected that they would die of cold in the autumn weather. Later, soldiers armed with tommy guns were given the task of shooting escaping animals. Although these arrangements sound inhuman, Belle Vue received favourable treatment, as the Company was able to satisfy the Emergency Committee and Chief Constable that the danger posed by such animals was slim, in view of the high perimeter walls.

Permission to reopen, received on the afternoon of Friday 15th September, was too late to allow adequate publicity to be mounted and only a trickle of visitors came the following day. No-one was admitted without a gasmask. The firework displays had ended by September and both the Railway Carnival and September Band Contest were cancelled. The latter was afterwards held on 30th September, but transport difficulties led to a reduced audience and an early finish. Only eight bands appeared out of twenty-three entered. Speedway was interrupted, but quickly resumed. It was not affected by wartime fuel restrictions as the machines used wood alcohol as fuel, referred to as "dope". Boxing and wrestling matches were immediately stopped and Broughton Rangers did not play again until 1945. Professor le Fay worked out the remainder of his contract.

Belle Vue was inundated with animals from other zoos which had been forced to close early in the war. Also, many members of the public wanted the Zoo to

The Zoo in wartime: a tapir being fed on stale bread and vegetables in November 1940

look after pets, because Belle Vue had a priority supply of animal foods. This favourable situation did not last for long and by November prices had risen considerably; certain foods became unobtainable soon afterwards.

The outbreak of war also caused problems for the Christmas Circus. Many acts were marooned abroad and acts from Germany could not appear. The arrangements for the circus fell almost entirely on ringmaster George Lockhart. The 1939/40 season was cut to three weeks and then extended by a week. The customary show for under-privileged children was not given. The imposition of black-out restrictions caused some difficulties, but subdued strip lighting was arranged between the Kings Hall and the Hyde Road entrance and the Corporation ran certain buses direct from the door of the Hall.

In June 1940 evacuees from Dunkirk were given meals at Belle Vue, organised by the management, and the escape of the British Forces was commemorated by a Service of Thanksgiving in the Stadium. About this time members of the local Home Guard were issued with 1866 vintage Snyder rifles from the firework display armoury. Substantial efforts were made to get the 1940 season operating as normally as possible, and there was a record Easter attendance, blessed by good weather. Serving members of the Forces were admitted for half price.

The children's rides, Seaplanes and Jack and Jill, did not operate and the firework displays were replaced by a series of indoor entertainments. Bonelli arranged a Vaudeville show, the Belle Vue Follies, in the Kings Hall; a "Tudor Cabaret" was laid on and the Manchester Mill Girl Pipers Band appeared. Professor le Fay appeared in the Japanese Tea Room. At Whitsuntide, a concert party entertainment, the Belle Vue Revels, was organised in the Kings Hall. A show put on by trick cyclists, "Sky Walkers and Human Spiders", appeared for August Bank Holiday. The Zoo Shop continued to function and in June 1940 its entire stock of toy animals was bought by a family of refugees.

The Blitz of the winter of 1940/1 meant that the Circus was carried out in very difficult conditions. Rehearsals were interrupted and some acts couldn't make it for the opening on Christmas Eve because of the heavy bombing raids a few days earlier. The acts that appeared included Pepino and his miniature circus, a delightful music hall act which returned to Belle Vue on a semi-permanent basis years later.

Only a few hundred turned up to the first performance and shows were restricted to afternoons, although two evening performances were tried, without success. Nevertheless, the fact that the Circus had been put on at all was a success, as there was only one other circus in the country that year. Bonelli had difficulty in getting suitable musicians, and even those he could obtain were usually employed in munitions work and either had to arrive late for performances or leave early.

In the Zoo, 1940 saw many difficulties. Some foods, such as bananas, had disappeared altogether, and fish was hard to get. The sealions were coaxed to take strips of beef soaked in cod liver oil, on which they apparently thrived, but they died later of stomach ulcers. The lions were enthusiastic about green-coloured horsemeat, as were the monkeys about boiled potatoes, but the lack of millet seed and other foods caused the loss of the birds of paradise, and the penguins died too. Once again, lettuce, cabbages and carrots were grown in the Kitchen Gardens, and canary seed was later tried.

By 1943 all but three of the keepers had been called up and the Zoo had to rely on casual workers, some of whom had to be dismissed for stealing horse-meat intended for the lions. No bombs fell on the Gardens, although the centre of the scenic railway was hit by an incendiary. The Reptile House was damaged by shell splinters from ack-ack guns, which also caused the death of a bull bison. Maintenance of buildings was suspended and one winter a giraffe named Mary died after the roof of the Camel House partially collapsed. Further animal losses occurred when the heating of the aviary, aquarium, lion and monkey

A late World War II photograph of the two-foot-high "Wee Beauty", claimed to be the world's smallest pony. It came to Belle Vue from Belfast Zoo

houses was affected by a strike at the Corporation's gasworks. Among the fatalities were the lioness Pearl and her litter of cubs. Most of the tropical fish died when an inexperienced foreman plumber shut off the gas supply by mistake.

Some replacement animals arrived and in 1940 the reptile collection of Paignton Zoo's Herbert Whitley was presented to Belle Vue. August 1940 saw the arrival of Hercules, a 150-year-old tortoise. The break up of Sanger's Circus in September 1941 led to the purchase of the Indian elephant Annie for 50 guineas. The male tigon, Kliou, died shortly after Easter 1941.

The war had a significant effect on Company finances. The profit for the year ending October 1939 was only £1,217, and that for the following year £2,576. The Company claimed compensation for the requisitioned facilities: £4,000 was obtained in 1941 and £7,242 in 1942, although a mobile canteen was presented to the Civil Defence services. In 1941 the Corporation requisitioned parts of the Hyde Road and Redgate Lane car parks, together with the Kirkmanshulme House site, for use as allotments. George Wilson died in January 1941 and was replaced by H F B Iles. The speedway manager, E O Spence, became Managing Director, his place being taken by his secretary, Miss A S Hart.

Surprisingly, several developments were carried out in 1941. The Leopard House, now called the Small Cat House, was converted to an amusement arcade, and there were changes to the Hyde Road Hotel, now called the Palm Court Hotel. Dividing walls on the ground floor were taken down and a large hall was formed to hold concerts in the winter months. Professor le Fay's shows continued to be successful and were moved to a larger area in the Popular Restaurant. By 1941 both boxing and wrestling matches had been resumed, although the promotion of either was difficult because of the high level of Entertainment Duty imposed on all but charity matches. The 1941 Circus took place under better conditions, but George Lockhart had to manage with ring girls instead of his usual team of boys, a change which proved to be quite successful.

Substantial alterations were carried out to the Aviary and Lion House in January 1942, many of the cages being completely rebuilt. In April, a Grand Festival of Massed Bands and Choirs was held in aid of Mrs Churchill's Aid to Russia Fund, at which appeared the Black Dyke Mills, Foden's Motor Works, Fairey Aviation and the Besses o'th'Barn Bands. In June, a Battle for Freedom Pageant was held, featuring Sir Malcolm Sargent and Lieutenant Laurence Olivier, RNVR. In August, free concerts were given by the Belle Vue Forces Music Club, run by Gerald Iles. At first, this used gramophone records, but later concerts were given by the Manchester Women's String Orchestra, the Gorton Philharmonic Society and soloists such as the soprano Isobel Baillie. Later that month, a series of marching contests started in the stadium, the first event attracting an audience of 10,000, and eleven bands, five from the Home Guard. The presence of US forces in the area led to a baseball match in the stadium that month. Following an outcry, a meeting of Jehovah's Witnesses, who were opposed to war, was cancelled on the orders of the Home Secretary.

E O Spence, Speedway Manager 1929-41 and Managing Director 1941-47

By now the value of the Gardens as a place of wartime entertainment was realised. People were encouraged to take holidays at home and increased attendances followed. The profits for the year ending October 1941 had risen to £7,752. The children's amusement park had reopened by 1943, but the main funfair was restricted to ten rides, a situation which persisted throughout the war. The most popular ride was the Caterpillar, and another one of these was installed later.

An additional locomotive was obtained for the Miniature Railway in 1943 and, with the shortage of manpower, an appeal was made for retired loco drivers. The locomotive, known simply as No.3, was originally "Synolda", supplied to the estate railway of Sir Robert Walker at Sand Hutton near York in 1912. It was named "Prince Charles" in the early 1950s. Professor le Fay put in another appearance in 1943, this time next to the Bobs. The Battle for Freedom pageant was repeated in 1943. For a time, the Exhibition Hall held a small number of German POWs.

Miss Hart, the UK's first female Speedway Manager (from 1941 to 1952), with mechanics

Sammy, the red fox who had evaded capture since 1937, was finally caught napping on the roof of one of the greenhouses, where he was put to rest with the aid of a bullet. His skin was made into a fur for the wife of one of the directors. In July, Gerald Iles announced that all new animals to the Gardens were to be named after celebrities. A Home Guard assault took place on Firework Island in May. At the end of the year, the Pagoda restaurant was requisitioned as a sorting office to deal with the Christmas post.

In February 1944 Gerald Iles appeared in "News from the Manchester Zoo", the first of many Children's Hour broadcasts.

Easter 1944 broke all records and 179,000 visitors passed through the turnstiles on Easter Monday. Anyone wishing to ride the Caterpillar, Bobs or Scenic Railway had a three-quarter-hour wait. Troops were admitted free of charge. In August, a grand March of Liberty Festival was organised, attended by Herbert Morrison, and in September, the Daily Herald sponsored a March for Freedom display, in which ten bands and 1,000 voices took part, as well as fifteen National Service bands. John Henry Iles appeared as conductor, his affairs of the past apparently forgotten, following his receipt of an OBE that year. During the August Bank Holiday, the open air dancing platform was used for the first time in four years.

In December 1944 the Manchester Labour Party published proposals for post war development and reconstruction of the city. Its controversial agenda contained a plan to take Belle Vue under municipal control. The Zoo was to be the Northern equivalent of Regents Park, and the whole complex would be extended towards the city as far as Ardwick Green. New exhibition buildings, a boating pool, lido, wave bath, planetarium and a first class stadium would be provided, the various components of the Gardens being linked by a system of internal railways. A bid would be made to stage the first Olympic Games there after the war. The proposals were not well received; the official Corporation Post War Reconstruction Committee thought that the Labour Party had usurped its own responsibilities, and a Company official dryly remarked that they had received no approaches from the Corporation about the possible purchase of the Gardens.

"Prince Charles", the third locomotive acquired for the Miniature Railway, seen here in the mid-1950s

Easter 1945 drew near record crowds, over 173,000 passing through the turnstiles on Easter Monday. Many new amusements were introduced, including the second Caterpillar ride and Over the Falls. Other rides closed for the war were re-opened. Wee Beauty, the world's smallest pony, 24 inches high, from Belfast, was on display, together with Ronnie, a three-legged rooster. April saw the appointment of D Buckland Smith as Press and Publicity Director. For the previous seven years he had been Press Director and Assistant Manager of the Manchester Hippodrome. Mr Smith featured prominently in Belle Vue's affairs for over ten years.

The end of the year was celebrated in festive style. The Hyde Road entrance was covered in flags of the United Nations and the Avenue was decorated with illuminations. An illuminated Cinderella's coach was provided for children's rides, and Over the Falls was decorated with a huge effigy of Stalin, as a tribute to the country's wartime ally. The Amusement Park remained open until 2.00am on VE Day.

J H Iles presenting the "Class B" Cup at the 1944 Marching Band Contest

The Halle Orchestra 1942-72

The Halle Orchestra had been looking for a suitable concert hall since the Free Trade Hall was blitzed on the night of

22nd December 1940. Concerts were held in theatres, cinemas, and the Albert Hall on Peter Street, but these either lacked the necessary acoustic qualities or were too small. The orchestra first made use of the Coronation Ballroom for a recording session in 1941. An experimental concert was held in the Kings Hall on 12th April 1942, with Leslie Heward conducting Cyril Smith in the Grieg Piano Concerto and other works. Conditions were rather hot and the instruments had to be retuned frequently. Another concert was held in June and the Messiah was given at Christmas, but the Orchestra's management was still undecided about Belle Vue's suitability as a venue.

The Halle was obliged to give the matter serious consideration when in 1943 the City Council decided to permit the opening of cinemas on Sundays, thus depriving the orchestra of venues for its popular Sunday concerts. The Halle had undergone something of a transformation that year, coinciding with the appointment of John Barbirolli as conductor. The first performance of the reformed orchestra under Barbirolli took place in the Kings Hall on 15th August 1943 and Granville Hill, music critic of the Manchester Guardian, described it as "orchestral playing finer than we have heard in Manchester for many years".

The Company is said to have made the hall available on an expenses-only basis. The acoustics were considered to be remarkably good, despite the occasional roar of a lion in the distance, the noise of the Amusement Park or the twittering of sparrows caught in the roof. Most of all, the place had an intimate atmosphere, with the orchestra in the centre instead of the normal concert arrangement. Barbirolli used George Lockhart's changing room, which had "Ringmaster" on the door. Sir Malcolm Sargent, who often conducted the annual "Messiah", used the same room, as did Pablo Casals, when he played there in 1945. The "Messiah" performances had to be fitted in with the Christmas Circuses, and Sargent recalled that once, whilst taking the applause at the end of the "Messiah", he caught sight of some elephants waiting outside. Trained to give a bow on hearing applause, the elephants were bowing away out of sight of any audience.

The 1944/45 season at Belle Vue included a performance of Verdi's "Requiem", dedicated to the memory of the late President F D Roosevelt. The number of concerts given at Belle Vue in 1946 was cut from 22 to 16 as the Company wanted to extend the opening of the Amusement Park, which they had been obliged to curtail during performances, following complaints. Even then, one member of the audience took matters into his own hands in October, mounted the platform during the interval and urged the audience to write to the Belle Vue management about the noisy interruptions of the Scenic Railway. Although he found some support, he was given a frosty reply by the Halle management and Barbirolli saw no cause for complaint. They had no other option, of course, for to pursue the matter might have left the orchestra without a hall for its Sunday concerts.

KING'S HALL
BELLE VUE, MANCHESTER
Sir
Ralph
Richardson
will be the orator in
"MORNING HEROES"
(BLISS)
with the
HALLE ORCHESTRA
and CHOIR
Conductor: HERBERT BARDGETT
SUNDAY, 16th APRIL, at 6-30 p.m.
The programme also includes
Homage March .... Grieg
Capriccio Espagnol .... Rimsky-Korsakov
Fantasia on Greensleeves .... Vaughan Williams
Prince Igor (with choir) .... Borodin
Ticket Prices 7/6 6/- 5/- 4/- 2/6
★ 20% REDUCTION IN TICKET PRICES WILL BE GIVEN FOR PARTIES OF TWENTY OR MORE
All enquiries to
HALLÉ BOOKING OFFICE, 8, St. Peter's Square, Manchester, 2
CENtral 2023

Halle advertisement from 1950

The Halle used Belle Vue only for the first four Sunday concerts of its 1951/2 season as the Free Trade Hall was re-opened in November 1951. But the link was not broken that easily and by January 1952 a partial return was being considered. The new Free Trade Hall was not large enough to allow the orchestra to make a financial surplus on its popular concerts, and a number of Sunday concerts were again held in the Kings Hall. The "Messiah", too, continued at Belle Vue, and on 7th December 1952 the legendary Kathleen Ferrier sang her last ever "Messiah". The Halle Orchestra continued to give concerts at Belle Vue in the later 1950s and thereafter they were restricted to the Christmas "Messiah", the Halle Christmas Ball in the Cumberland Suite and the occasional children's concert. After 1972, even the "Messiah" was transferred to the Free Trade Hall.

Although a relatively short period in the history of either institution, the connection of Belle Vue and the Halle had been notable. In the late 1940s, shortly after he had received an invitation to be conductor of one of the London orchestras, Barbirolli, when taking the rapturous applause at the Kings Hall one evening, said to his wife Evelyn, "How can I leave that?"

Post War Prosperity 1945-50

With the end of the war the Zoo resumed its acquisitions, although at first these were restricted to animals already in the country. A number of purchases were made from private collections, and an alligator was bought from Regents Park. Shortly afterwards, some Pere David's deer and a bull bison were acquired from the Duke of Bedford at Woburn.

Other aspects began to return to normal, and although no firework displays were held that year, the traditional burning of Guy Fawkes was resumed. This time the figure possessed clothes made out of old blackout cloth, had a 3½ft-high hat and stood on a bonfire covering 24 sq ft. Broughton Rangers were re-formed. At the Company's request, the Gorton Philharmonic Society agreed to hold an evening concert in place of its customary "open rehearsal". This alteration was a success, resulting in better attendances and improved orchestral playing. The concerts for October 1945, and three concerts the following year, were held in the evening, as were all subsequent performances.

In late September, in addition to the usual Brass Band Contest, sections of the Daily Herald National Brass Band Competition, normally held in London, took place. The "Victory Circus" was held over four weeks that year. In order to help out with a record Christmas Post in 1945, two of the cafes became temporary sorting offices.

In the previous July there had been rumours that Billy Butlin, the holiday camp magnate, was interested in the Gardens. Both the Belle Vue Board and Butlin denied this and the rumours were dismissed as an attempt to raise the Company's share prices. By December 1944 the deferred ordinary shares, worth 1d each in 1942, had risen to 10/-, but much of the increase was explained by the record admissions enjoyed over the previous three years. Payment of arrears on the preferred ordinary shares had now been made up to February 1938, and it was proposed that arrears on these shares up to October 1944 should also be paid. To enable this, a resolution had to be passed at an Extraordinary General Meeting of the Company.

Held in March 1945, this meeting was the opportunity that the Company's critics had been waiting for. Many of the smaller shareholders had been agitated since the 1930s and by 1944 the troubles had attracted the interest of larger scale financiers, who saw the possibility of acquiring control of the Company and so began buying shares. Led by a Manchester insurance broker, J M Moody, the rebel shareholders managed to secure representation on the Board by the appointment of a Mr J McLaren. The group claimed to control over half the deferred ordinary shares, which were rumoured to have been the former holdings of John Henry Iles. Demands were made for the removal of H F B Iles and three other directors. Allegations were made that the Board's failure to pay interest for 1944/45 on the preferred ordinary shares was "vexatious". Shareholders received circulars from both sides and threats of legal action were mentioned in the press. However, at the April Annual General Meeting the Board won a tactical victory. McLaren was voted off, but it was not the end of the matter.

D Buckland Smith, Belle Vue's flamboyant Press and Publicity Director from 1945 to 1956

The boardroom battles had little effect on the continued development of the Gardens. In January 1946 Buckland Smith established his own Press and Publicity Department. This had a bill posting section, photographers, special telephone links with newspapers, etc, and the whole level of publicity vastly increased. Over 100 photographs were sent out to newspapers daily and advertisements were placed in 175 local

Broughton Rangers about to depart for an away fixture, some time between their re-formation in 1945 and the change of name to Belle Vue Rangers in October 1946

papers, mainly in the two week period preceding each town's Wakes Week. Contact was maintained with 1,800 bus and coach operators. In time for Easter, a two months campaign was launched involving 500 bill posting sites, the issue of 1,500 photographs and a 30-page brochure entitled "Showground of the World".

In anticipation of record Easter crowds, the Gardens opened at 9.00am and twelve extra turnstiles were erected. There were 250,000 visitors by Easter Monday. New attractions included a Lilliputian Fair, a Verbeck Street Organ and an animated robot show in the old Fish Restaurant building. The Amusement Park contained the Brownie Coaster, Cakewalk, two Caterpillars, Ferris Wheel, Ghost Train, Hall of Laughter, Hurricane Racer, Kiddies' Roundabouts, Merry-Go-Round, Midget Car Racing, Moon Rocket, Octopus, Over the Falls, Punch and Judy, Skooters, See-Saw, Tumblebug and the Wall of Death ride, as well as slot machine arcades.

A ride on the Bobs, July 1946. The sailors were from destroyers moored on the Ship Canal

Queues at the Hyde Road entrance in 1946. The tramlines in the foreground were part of the siding which was laid for horse trams by the family in 1880. The lines could still be seen in the 1980s

By April 1946 the Exhibition Hall was still being used by the War Office for storage, although the Company soon regained possession for a machine tools exhibition. In June, a 25-mile cycle race was held on the internal roadways of the Gardens. July saw visits of sailors from the destroyers Zealous, Zest and Zambesi, moored on the Ship Canal for an official visit to the city. It is said that on one of the many visits to Belle Vue by navy men, havoc was caused at the River Caves ride. Participants were taken in small boats past various tableaux, one of which comprised stuffed animals, including a tiger, from the old Museum. On the sailors' second trip round, some of the animals were put in one of the boats, causing bystanders to take fright when it returned to the entrance.

In August, a solo Brass Championship was held, organised by the Daily Herald. At the suggestion of playwright George Bernard Shaw, several old instruments were played by acknowledged experts. Jack Mackintosh played the slide trumpet, Alec Mortimer the ophicleide and Harry Mortimer, who was to be involved with the Brass Band Contests for decades to come, played Handel's aria "O Ruddier than the Cherry" on a keyed bugle. Over 200,000 visited the Gardens over August Bank Holiday.

In September, some of Belle Vue's rowing boats were used during serious flooding in Salford. A special speedway meeting was held, featuring Professor Lowe with a rocket-propelled motorcycle, which raised £105 for the Mayor of Salford's Flood Relief Fund. The Gardens featured in a civic film, "A City Speaks", directed by Paul Rotha. The Fireworks were revived, but without the battlepieces, because of the shortage of building materials and the need to get special government licences for building projects. Only eight men were used for the display, which included a replica of a large golden waterfall, 260ft long and 26ft high, together with a royal portrait 28ft high. Certain Home Office restrictions on the use of chemicals had to be observed and there were no "big bangs".

In October, the Company's long standing mortgage debentures were paid off through the issue of 175,000 cumulative first preference shares. The issue was oversubscribed, a clear indication of confidence in the Gardens. A S Hart, the Speedway manager, was appointed to the Board and Broughton Rangers was renamed Belle Vue Rangers.

Additions to the Zoo continued to be made. Two giraffes were acquired for £250 each, and animals were bought from the trapper H R Stanton, who had brought them from Mombasa aboard the Clan Line steamer "Samderwent". Senior keeper James Craythorne had retired in 1944 and he was replaced by Matt Kelly, whose family had been involved with Dublin's Phoenix Park Zoo.

At the beginning of 1947, rumours of Billy Butlin's interest in Belle Vue surfaced again and were at first denied. However, there was more foundation to the story this time as Butlin acquired an interest in Margate Estates, the owner of Dreamland, also controlled by H F B Iles. Speculation sent the Belle Vue ordinary shares, on which no dividend had ever been paid, up to a giddy price of over 20/- each.

By July 1947 a deal had been thrashed out and Butlin was allowed to buy 200,000 new "A" deferred ordinary shares, which would not rank for dividend until 1949. Both Butlin and his chairman, Ian Anderson, gained seats on the Board. The new arrangement was welcomed by the Moody-McLaren group of rebel shareholders and this, together with the announcement of a dividend on the deferred ordinary shares, ended the dissent for the time being. Although Ian Anderson remained on the Board for many years, Butlin soon gave up his place because of other commitments. At no time did he plan to develop Belle Vue into a residential holiday village and most of his other ideas could not be put into effect because of the continued restrictions on building.

1947 started badly owing to an exceptionally cold winter. The reptile collection and some birds had to be kept in special rooms closed to the public to maintain warmth. Gerald Iles looked after some snakes in his flat. In March the elephant Lil, which had come with Phil Fernandez in 1921, died aged 50.

Easter that year was wet, although a crowd of 165,000 turned up on Easter Monday. Over 2,000 coaches crowded the surrounding streets and demands were made that the Corporation and the Company do something about the problem. The answer would have been for the Corporation to surrender land requisitioned for allotments, but after representations from the allotment holders, this plan was dropped.

Attractions laid on for 1947 included the Great Omi, a tattooed man, and the Globe Infernal, featuring Lauri Staig and the Hell Drivers. In the latter, racing motorcycles were ridden on the inside of a globe. New boats were placed on the lakes, including a replacement for the Little Eastern, the last of the Jennison paddle steamers.

An unusual innovation was the conversion of the Penguin House for an attraction named Frogmen Divers. Three demobilised midget submarine officers had formed a company called Universal Divers to secure contracts for underwater work. To raise money for the necessary equipment, they put on a show in the 40ft-long glass-sided tank of the Penguin House. They constructed a replica of a midget sub airlock, and the public saw the divers getting through this airlock with equipment to make their way through mock obstruction nets. The show was a success and continued until 1952. The divers also did some long overdue clearance work in the ponds in the Gardens and helped recover a dead girl from a pond in Denton.

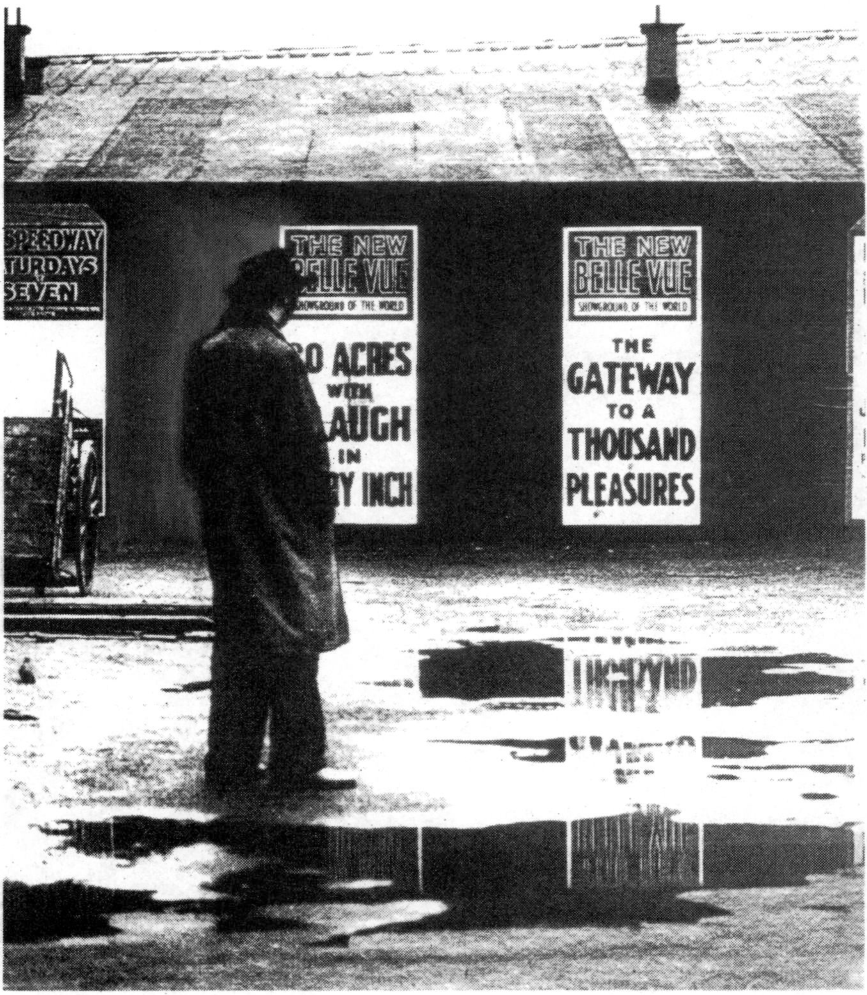

1946 - some of "Buckland's" posters

The penguins displaced by the divers were given part of the Rocky Mountain Enclosure, where a new pool was built. A consignment of 20 penguins arrived in August to replace 17 which had recently died of disease. Earlier in the year, Belle Vue had its first sealions for seven years, and other losses of the war years were replaced. The old outdoor Sea-lion Pool was not re-used and was later filled in. The South Terrace and Beaver Pond also remained unused.

In May the Evening Chronicle organised a Youth Rally, including a Sports Brains' Trust featuring Matt Busby among others. In September the Railway Carnival was revived and a new scenic artist, Syd Lane, was appointed. That month there was an experiment by the Rediffusion Company to bring television, then only being received in London, to Manchester. An aircraft containing a television flew at a height of 300-400ft above the Gardens, successfully picking up the transmission from London. It was hoped to install a tower aerial, or to suspend an aerial from a balloon at a similar height, and to relay broadcasts to viewing rooms at Belle Vue. The rapid expansion of the television network soon overtook this idea.

September 1947 saw the death of the managing director, E O Spence. He was replaced by the secretary, Richard Morton Dixon. The post of secretary was taken over by Thomas Gerard Nolan.

The Zoological Superintendent and his staff in the late 1940s

Winston Churchill spoke in the Kings Hall in December and the Christmas Circus was extended for a record run, being seen by over 400,000 people. The Railway Queen appeared at one of the early performances, arriving in the arena aboard a train on the Miniature Railway. This had been extended into the Kings Hall for the performance to celebrate the nationalisation of the railways.

1948 saw several developments in the Zoo. The first of these was Gerald Iles's successful acquisition of a gerenuk, or giraffe-necked gazelle, called Gerry, which was housed in a special compartment in the Camel, Giraffe and Rhino House. This addition was a real scoop, as no such animal had been kept in this country before. Iles had been searching for one for ten years. Gerry proved a useful attraction for the next two years until he died of pneumonia. The 1948 Christmas Circus featured a show put on by the sealion trainer, "Captain" Harry Smith. His sea-lions dutifully mounted pedestals, played with a giant ball, juggled with lighted tapers, played trumpets and one even drove a miniature car. Captain Smith and his wife Evelyn were Germans (named Schmidt) and they had looked after the Sealion House since the reintroduction of sea-lions the previous year. Their act proved a popular addition to the Circus over the next few years.

The Aviary at the southern end of the Paddock House was converted into the Hall of Living Jewels, or Jewelhouse, over the winter of 1948/49. Adapting an idea he had seen in New York, Gerald Iles wished to display to greater effect the exotic and brightly coloured small birds of the Zoo. Thus humming birds, sunbirds, birds of paradise, etc, were placed in ten compartments containing tropical plants. The public viewed the birds from a darkened corridor, which helped to highlight the beauty of the birds and also discouraged them from flying into the glass fronts. Each compartment had an upper section to which the birds could gain access, and behind the whole display was a large

Matt Kelly with members of the Busy Bee Club, October 1948

cage where the birds could rest. Iles later thought that the cage was not needed and used it instead for small mammals. Unfortunately the display did not prove a great attraction and the public tended to walk past the door or spent little time viewing the small, richly coloured birds.

The prosperity of the post war years is reflected in the extra funfair amusements provided. Although one of the Caterpillar rides had gone, along with the Cakewalk, an Autodrome had appeared, together with the Skid. New sideshows included Madame Astra (Palmiste), Pandora's Box, Jolli Snaps, Recording Discs, Prince Kari Karl's Jungle Fantasy and Rasool Haraza's Pakistani Theatre. This last was located in the old Jennison amusements area behind the Lion House. The old First Class Tea Room had by now been demolished.

The surviving tigon, Maude, died of gastro-enteritis when the heating plant failed in the Lion House in December 1949. On March 27th 1950 the elephant Annie was persuaded to hold a Union Jack outside the Hyde Road entrance, next to a line of keepers, when the young Princess Margaret passed by on her way to lay the foundation stone of the new Free Trade Hall. On the Miniature Railway, the locomotive "Railway Queen" was given a new boiler and additional fire escapes were provided in the Kings Hall. At the end of the year, the heating system of the Reptile House failed, causing the death of a great reticulated python and seriously affecting some other snakes.

By 1950 the Company's financial position had worsened. The post war boom had slackened off and profits (£30,968 in 1946, £45,523 in 1947 and £41,847 in 1948) dropped to £17,372. To keep up confidence, the Board continued to pay a high dividend to the deferred ordinary shareholders, who received their very first dividend of 25% in 1946, and 50% in the following two years. The 1950 dividend was only 15%. It must have been frustrating for the Company to see this situation arise, for they had been unable to accumulate the profits earned in the years of prosperity through the imposition of Excess Profits and Entertainment Taxes. Nor could the profits be channelled into improvements and rebuilding as these were still regulated by the building licensing system.

Years of Uncertainty 1951-56

Early in 1951 the Company rebuilt and modernised the Exhibition Hall Restaurant. Previously this was a barn-like affair, in effect an extension of the Hall itself. The new restaurant was a more manageable size, capable of seating 1,500. A new floor and platform were laid and a smaller restaurant, the Belfast, constructed alongside.

John Henry Iles died in May, aged 79. Apart from the Band Contests, he had played little part in running the Gardens since 1938. Although he had promised that he would rebuild his lost fortune, he remained with brass band journalism, managing to buy back the British Bandsman. His editorials in this were always headed with the apt description, "From the Chief".

In January 1951 Gerald Iles made his first TV appearance in the programme "For the Children", in which several zoo animals, sketched by the artist Harry Rutherford, were shown. Several improvements were undertaken in 1951. New parrot cages were completed inside the Aviary. These contained new drinking containers intended to be unbreakable, but the parrots managed to undo them in due course. A long overdue re-roofing of the Monkey House was carried out and in December, similar repairs to the Aquarium and Reptile House commenced. The fish were given temporary accommodation under the Firework Stand and no more reptiles were acquired until the repairs were complete. Meanwhile, there had been mysterious losses of snakes from the outdoor Reptilium. Apparently one of the Zoo's large domestic cat population, Sue, was undaunted by the risk of being poisoned by the deadly snakes and was stealing and killing them. Sue was found a new home at a public house in Middleton, where she was quite happy.

In September 1951 Gerald Iles proposed a series of outdoor enclosures next to the Paddock House for long horned species such as bison. Four months later he announced plans to rebuild the Monkey Terrace, but neither proposal could be

Lion-tamer "Dolas" at the 1949/50 Circus

implemented because of the tight fiscal situation.

On April 12th 1952 the BBC made its first outside broadcast from Belle Vue, transmitting to aerials on top of Ship Canal House in the city centre. Gerald Iles gave a commentary, but the event was a disaster, caused partly by the heavy, incessant rain. The same month there was a fire in a sideshow named African Fantasy. 13,000 rounds of ammunition, two snakes and part of the adjacent Bobs were destroyed. A third snake was rescued through the bravery of a 27-year-old African girl, Ali Matu, who was featuring in the show.

In May 1952 the Corporation gave up many of its allotment sites on the car parks, although it retained the Kirkmanshulme House site and a small area off Belle Vue Avenue until about 1960.

New attractions were introduced for the 1952 season in an effort to revive attendances. On Firework Island a Swiss, Herr Buhlman, described as the "V2 Rocket Man", shot out of a barrel at 120mph and up a ramp nine yards long. At the top of the ramp the rocket opened into four parts and its occupant was thrown into a net. Also on the island, a team of Australian Air Aces from the Wall of Death rode motorcycles which revolved a steel-framed trapeze, on which three performers executed a series of aerial gymnastics. Another act involved an acrobat ascending a swaying pole, 100 feet high, on top of which he placed a ladder and at the top of this was a chair. In October, Syd Lane completed a 32ft by 12ft mural over the Hyde Road staff entrance, showing two dozen animals, and a smaller mural over the Palm Court Hotel entrance. The effectiveness of his work was all too rapidly diminished by the acid Manchester atmosphere.

GERALD ILES AND TWO OF HIS PETS

Gerald Iles with lion cubs Samson and Delilah, on a greetings postcard of the early 1950s

Johnnie Hoskins, Speedway Manager from 1953 until 1961. He introduced the sport to the UK in 1928

In the early 1950s the Kings Hall saw many events. Bob Hope appeared in 1951; Nye Bevan, Gilbert Harding, Lena Horne and Gracie Fields all appeared in 1952. The Press and Publicity Manager, D Buckland Smith, absent in 1951 through illness, produced a comic called Circus Fun for the 1951/52 Circus, 25,000 copies of which were sold.

The veteran elephant Annie died in July 1952. In the same month, a new Zoo Shop was opened, manned by 20-year-old Frank Woolhams, to whom Iles gave the task of "Zoo Answers Man" - to answer questions put to staff by children about animals. The repairs to the aquarium were finally completed in November and the tanks were restocked. In all, 80 species of fish were displayed and given better illumination by the introduction of infra red and ultra violet lighting. At the Circus that year, Gerald Iles introduced an act named Noah's Ark, consisting of Zoo animals including two elephants, Ram Moti and Ram Khali, a llama, goat, cockatoo, two camels and a cycling chimp named Suzy. This was an idea of R M Dixon, but it was presented as an extension of Iles's educational and publicity work, although it is possible that the use of the Zoo animals was also an economy measure. Still, the comparison between zoo and circus animals must have been interesting.

The Speedway manager, Alice Hart, left at the end of 1952 and was replaced by the veteran speedway promoter, Johnnie

Hoskins. The appointment of the Aces' arch rival raised a few eyebrows at the time, but Hoskins was quickly accepted by both team and fans. Frank Parker, the manager of the Brass Band Contests, died in January 1953, ending a family connection with the contests that went back to the 1860s. A Frank Parker Trophy was introduced to the contest that year. The May and July contests were amalgamated in 1954 to form the Spring Brass Band Festival, held in May. Frank Parker's place was taken by Jack Fearnley, who had been appointed as Business Development Manager in 1951. He had earlier played with Belle Vue Rangers and had been involved on the catering side of Belle Vue.

Syd Lane working on his portraits of the Queen and Duke of Edinburgh, May 1953

To commemorate the Coronation in 1953, a special display was arranged on the floral clock at the Hyde Road entrance. Over £90,000 was spent on repairs. Business improved following the modernisation of some of the kitchens, but 1953 was not a good year for the Company; profits fell from £13,081 in 1952 to an all-time low of £1,915. This was blamed on bad summer weather and on the growing influence of television. The increasing availability of consumer goods and the impact of the Coronation with its attendant street parties, together with the large number of televisions bought or rented to view the Coronation ceremony, meant that the public had less money to spend on other entertainment. Although catering, exhibitions and circus receipts had improved, boxing and wrestling attendances were down and receipts were hit by the imposition of higher Entertainment Tax.

Hungry hippos in the old outdoor pool next to the Elephant House

Some shareholders levelled criticism particularly at the Zoo, where feeding costs averaged £250 a week. It was suggested that the Zoo be closed completely, or the animals lent to fairgrounds for display at pets' corners, then considered commercially attractive. These, together with more serious suggestions of holding a special committee of enquiry into the losses, or of selling up the site completely, were rejected by the Board, who announced plans to restage the Firework Display battlepieces, last seen in 1939, and proposals to introduce the new sport of stock car racing to the Stadium. The latter caused a rise in share prices, which added to the financial insecurity, as did rumours of another bid by Billy Butlin. Certainly, the profit levels did little to justify the speculation; the dividend on the deferred ordinary shares was only 10% for 1952 and there was no payment at all for 1953.

The financial gloom at the start of 1954 was not helped by a fire in the floor of the Coronation Ballroom. Easter was a success, however, with some 230,000 visitors between Good Friday and Easter Monday. In the Amusement Park, new rides included a Bubble Bounce and a Cyclodrome, the latter being a conversion of a roundabout called Noah's Ark. There was a visit by the miniature circus owned by the clown Pepino, which had been a successful show at fairgrounds and variety theatres. Pepino himself had appeared at the Christmas Circus during the war years. The little show had its own tent and featured a pony, monkey and four dogs. In one act, two terriers rode jockey on the back of the pony, a Great Dane acting as a mount. The show's finale featured the two terriers racing around the ring whilst a third terrier ran in the opposite direction and hurdled over them. The circus proved popular and Pepino appeared regularly in the summer months, and soon adopted Belle Vue as his semi-permanent home.

In July a pair of gerenuks arrived to replace Gerry, who died in 1950. They were housed in the old Penguin House, but their life at Belle Vue was comparatively short. In September a furore erupted over the acquisition of Aurora, a three-year-old polar bear, given by Chicago Zoo. When the unfortunate animal arrived in this country the authorities refused to grant an import licence. After adverse publicity and representations from Gerald Iles, officialdom backed down.

Two months later thieves broke into the Hall of Living Jewels and smashed cages, setting free five African sunbirds, an American robin and a £200 bird of paradise named Gorgeous George, who was to have featured with Iles in a TV broadcast in December. Other birds managed to get out of their compartments but were caught inside the Paddock House. The robin was eventually located and Gorgeous George was recaptured on the roof of the Camel and Giraffe House. Later the same month, Priscilla, a peahen, was found shot.

Stock car racing was introduced successfully by Johnnie Hoskins. The first meeting was held on 16th June 1954 and the season was extended to November. Hoskins had a reputation as something of a showman and there was little surprise when he introduced speedway fans to Johnnie's Marching Girls, a troupe of thirteen girls in red and white costumes who paraded at intervals in the meetings. The same girls took part in the battlepiece firework displays which restarted in 1954 with "The Storming of Quebec", made possible by the final lifting of wartime building controls. Months of preparation went into the displays, which lasted thirty minutes. 250 actors took part, mainly railwaymen, postal workers, army cadets and boy scouts, together with a few veterans of the old days. Produced by Christopher Ede, the display had synchronised sound tracks using the voices of professional actors. Buckland Smith claimed that the display was "Belle Vue's answer to television" and the show certainly was spectacular. The display's season was extended

A photograph taken at the first stock car meeting, 16th June 1954

R M Dixon, Managing Director 1947-56

because of its popularity. However, it was clear that such displays were no longer the money spinners they once were. The public now demanded a more sophisticated and therefore costly performance, and unlike the old days, it was necessary to pay the extras in cash rather than in beer and pies. Still, the Board was satisfied, for "The Relief of Lucknow" was organised for the following year.

The 1954/55 Christmas Circus was the first to be televised, the broadcast lasting 45 minutes. Contrary to expectations, ticket sales were boosted, although neither Gerald Iles nor Harry Smith appeared. On the whole, 1954 had seen a partial recovery of the Company's fortunes; profits after tax were £21,452 and a 10% dividend was paid. The weather had been favourable, and both the firework displays and stock car racing had been financially productive.

A Newsreel Theatre at the rear of the Kings Hall was provided in 1955, and work started on a new Children's Zoo next to the old Firework Factory, realising one of Gerald Iles's long standing plans. This cost £15,000 and was opened by the stage star Francis Lederer who, in the manner of the Pied Piper, led a crowd of children through the new attraction. It was built out of concrete, aluminium and plastic and contained an elaborate system of streams and pools. The biggest feature was a large concrete whale named "Willie", 32ft long and 8ft high, which contained a small aquarium. On the Redgate Lane side, a paddock area for zebra and Ankole cattle was provided.

1955 saw the death of James

The Hyde Road entrance in the early 1950s

Craythorne, the former veteran keeper of reptiles, who had continued to frequent the Gardens after his retirement in 1944. He was first employed at the Zoo in the 1880s at the age of 12 and followed in the footsteps of his father, who had been taken on some years earlier to look after the reptile collection. With his father, James undertook the preservation of the skeleton of the elephant Maharajah. James was greatly respected by George Jennison and it is said that he had been offered a job by Carl Hagenbeck. When he retired he was succeeded in the Reptile House by his son, Albert, who was followed by Clive Bennett in 1960.

The long-suffering Belle Vue Rangers were finally disbanded in August 1955 when their lease on the Stadium expired. Efforts were made to continue the club independent of Belle Vue, but Broughton Rangers (Belle Vue) Ltd was finally struck off the Companies Register in September 1959.

Involvement of the London Festival Gardens

The Company's financial problems reasserted themselves in 1955. H F B Iles, as Chairman of the Board, felt that something had to be done and early in 1956 he approached Sir Leslie Joseph. Sir Leslie had successfully organised the Festival of Britain amusement park in 1951 after being brought in by the then Labour Government at the last minute, and he had continued to run the Festival Gardens at Battersea Park.

In March 1956 he visited Belle Vue and the result was a virtual takeover by Sir Leslie and his associate, Charles Forte, who had run the catering concessions at the Festival Gardens. In a two-way transaction, Belle Vue acquired the latter and certain other interests of Joseph and Forte, who in return gained a controlling interest in Belle Vue through the transfer of 1,250,000 shares worth £87,000. H F B Iles remained as Chairman, but with only a nominal shareholding. Sir Leslie became Managing Director in place of R M Dixon and Charles Forte, Deputy Chairman. The takeover was considered by a special shareholders' meeting in July, when there was some opposition. One shareholder, a Dr Joseph Lurie of Manchester, suggested that the shareholders' interests would be better served if the Company went into liquidation and the assets, worth some £$\frac{3}{4}$m were realised. Fortunately he was outvoted.

The pre-1956 Company had been dogged by financial problems, apart from in the immediate post war years. Nevertheless, much had been achieved and successes like speedway, wrestling and the Circus far outweighed failures like the Cotton Pageant and Broughton Rangers. The role of Belle Vue during the war years was itself quite significant. As for the Zoo, the late 1940s and early 1950s were regarded as its zenith because of the breadth and variety of the collection kept under Gerald Iles.

The Gardens had undergone a vast change after the takeover from the Jennisons in 1925; a similar transformation was now to take place.

Phil Fernandez with Mary the elephant in 1953. Elephant rides were discontinued at Belle Vue about 1969

SIR LESLIE JOSEPH IN CONTROL 1956-63

Initial Changes 1956-58

A number of changes at managerial level were made immediately. The large Press and Publicity Department was drastically cut down and the services of the photographers discontinued. Buckland Smith was decidedly unhappy with this and resigned after a few months. His place was filled by Johnnie Hoskins, who combined the job with his Speedway duties. The catering manager, Harry Mitchell, was replaced by Ernest Davis, catering manager of the Festival Gardens, and the post of General Manager was recreated and filled by J W Betts, previously manager of the Festival Gardens.

Sir Leslie Joseph, Managing Director, set about reorganising Belle Vue along new lines. He was well qualified for the task. Between 1940 and 1946 he was president of the Association of Amusement Park Proprietors of Great Britain, and in the early 1950s he held posts with the National Amusements Council and the Amusements Caterers' Association. His knighthood was in recognition of his successes in 1951.

Many members of the old administration were retained. Gerald Iles remained in charge of the Zoo, T G Nolan as secretary, Jack Fearnley as business development manager and Dick Talbot, former assistant to R M Dixon, became assistant to Sir Leslie Joseph. The Zoo staff remained unaltered, although the death of Phil Fernandez in December caused some sadness.

The new management started redeveloping the Gardens at once. One of the first changes involved filling in a small part of the Great Lake, or Top Lake as it now became known, next to the Lake Hotel, where a small car park was formed. The Miniature Railway was uprooted from its position next to the Avenue to run from a new station between the Ballroom and the Firework Lake, passing the Aquarium and Reptile House and terminating behind the Lake Hotel on the banks of the Top Lake. The reasons for this change were twofold. First, the new station was located where the line could attract greater patronage, and secondly, the removal of the old line allowed the car park next to the Exhibition Hall to be segregated from the rest of the Gardens, thus preventing visitors to the Hall gaining free admission to the Gardens, and allowing the car park to be used exclusively for the Exhibition Hall. A new fence was built along the eastern side of The Avenue, and visitors to the Gardens from the Longsight entrance had to pass through a new set of turnstiles at the northern end of the Avenue. Close to the new turnstiles, a grassed area was laid out as an Enchanted Garden, incorporating an elevated Tree Walk over illuminated features, an idea which had been successful at the Festival Gardens.

The firework spectacle for 1956, "Robin Hood", arranged by the old management, was allowed to run its course, but it was not a financial success. Only ordinary displays were subsequently shown, though a running commentary continued to be provided. In the Stadium, Johnnie Hoskins introduced midget car racing again, this time with better success than in the 1930s. In October, Sir Leslie announced plans for a new Monkey House and a 60ft high cable car ride, level with the Scenic Railway. Some old amusements were discontinued, starting with the Hurricane Racer.

Redevelopment started in earnest in 1957, when the Centenary Gardens were swept away for a new water chute, completed for Easter. The components of the Centenary Gardens were erected elsewhere, the floral clock and the Gibbon Cage finding positions between the Ballroom and the Elephant House. The opportunity was taken to reposition the Gibbon Cage's internal house so keepers could gain easier and safer access. A new, smaller concrete enclosure for coypus was erected adjacent to the Elephant House on the site of the First Class Tea Room. Finally, the Monkey Mountain was replaced by Monkeyrama, which was located adjacent to the Scenic Railway in a corner of the Amusement Park. Monkeyrama comprised a large elliptical pit filled with concrete hexagonal shapes similar to a basalt formation. It was hoped that the presence of Javan monkeys would entice

The annual winter repainting of the Great Lake's rowing boats. The building in the background dates from 1863 and originally housed the steam hobby horses. Later it was used by Pepino's Circus

visitors into the Amusement Park.

The main Hyde Road turnstiles were altered early in 1957, being covered by a new metal structure, painted yellow and blue, designed by Oldham architects Tom Hayes & Partners, who were associated with Belle Vue throughout the remainder of its existence. Another alteration was the conversion of the old Leopard House, since 1942 an amusement arcade, into Louis Tussaud's Waxworks.

In July 1957 the Zoo acquired another tigon, a six-year-old female named Rita, originally owned by the Sultan of Morocco and acquired from the Paris Zoo at Vincennes in exchange for animals that Belle Vue obtained direct from Africa. Sir Leslie expressed concern over the cost of feeding the animals, which had risen tenfold since 1939, whereas admission charges had only doubled in the same period. Gerald Iles was obliged to introduce careful economies in the selection of animal food-stuffs.

Several attractions were laid on to extend the opening of the Amusement Park into the autumn. A race for waiters and waitresses was organised, together with a Treasure Hunt, charm contests, and a "yard of beer" drinking contest. During the summer the Gardens were plagued by a new phenomenon - the appearance of Teddy boys.

With the involvement of Charles Forte, greater emphasis was given to the development of the catering side of the business. In October 1957 the first of a series of "themed" catering outlets was opened, the Bavaria Banqueting Suite. Located in an old stable block, between the Bobs and the Hyde Road entrance, this had been converted at a cost of £30,000 and was provided with a sprung maple floor for dancing. The walls were adorned with murals painted by Syd Lane, showing mountain scenery and dancers. The new suite seated 250 diners and was officially opened by the Lord Mayor, Alderman Leslie Lever. At the same time, work started on converting the Pagoda Restaurant in the Ballroom block into an Elizabethan-style restaurant capable of seating 300.

October 1957 saw the departure of Gerald Iles to a job as director of a proposed 400-acre zoo at Montreal. The Zoo staff said their farewells at a ceremony in the Gardens attended by BBC officials and pianist Violet Carson. The restoration of Belle Vue to its position as premier provincial zoo had largely been Iles's doing, and he had brought dedication, knowledge, love of animals and perfectionism to the job. His reputation as a publicist was considerable and he had taken no fewer than 1,000 animals by taxi to the BBC's Manchester studios, had appeared in nearly 200 radio broadcasts and 20 TV broadcasts. His departure was not unexpected as control of the Gardens had passed from his family and he may have been apprehensive about working with the new management. On the other hand, there were ambitious plans for substantial reconstruction of the Zoo's outdated buildings and the time would have been ideal for Iles to achieve many of his ambitions, so often denied before 1956. As it turned out, the 400-acre zoo in Canada did not materialise and all he achieved was a modest children's zoo. He left the post after three years and became involved in organising wildlife expeditions to northern regions of Canada.

In November 1957 Sir Leslie announced plans for a Great Ape House and an enclosure for ruminants. A successor to Gerald Iles was quickly found and in December William Wilson from Craigend Castle, Milngavie, near Glasgow, was appointed. He came from a family of animal dealers and had run, albeit unsuccessfully, his own zoo at Craigend for a time. Shortly after his arrival, Wilson announced that the Zoo's future would be difficult financially, because rising costs were not being met by increased admission receipts. Also, increased car ownership meant that the Zoo's main competitor at Chester gained more customers than Belle Vue, having the added attraction of a journey through the Cheshire countryside.

The Ballroom Fire and the New Elizabethan Complex

In the early hours of 17th January 1958 a small fire started in the Ballroom block. Fanned by a south-westerly wind and aided by the wooden construction, the blaze spread to the entire block. A hundred firemen and twenty appliances arrived on the scene, but there was little that could be done. At the height of the blaze the prevailing wind caused the flames to lick the side of the Lion House and Aviary and there were fears for the animals inside, many of whom became alarmed. The birds were evacuated by Matt Kelly, his

The Firework Viewing Stand, located above the Ballroom Block

14-year-old son Bunny and William Wilson's daughter, Fiona, also 14. General Manager Jim Betts and Sir Leslie assisted in transferring the hundred or so birds to emergency quarters in the offices nearby. Transfer of most of the inmates of the Lion House was out of the question and on the orders of the Fire Chief, Wilson and a policeman armed themselves with rifles to shoot the animals. Judy, a 17-year-old lioness who was distressed, was shot, but further killing was not necessary. Firemen played their hoses over the roof of the building, forming a wall of water between it and the blazing Ballroom block and causing the temperature inside the Lion House to drop. When the Ballroom finally collapsed at about 3.30am, the wreckage came to within a foot of the Lion House.

The entire block was destroyed, including the Tudor Suite, Baronial Hall, Popular Cafe, York and American Bars, the fireworks viewing stand, a staff canteen, five shops and the Pagoda Restaurant, on which conversion work costing £40,000 had started. Also damaged beyond repair was the old outdoor dancing platform, little used since the war, although it had on occasions served as a skating rink. The total damage was estimated to be in the region of £250,000.

For insurance purposes, and to assist the Fire Brigade's investigations, the wreckage was left untouched for two weeks and formed an attraction for the curious. Two people suffered considerable personal loss. Many of Syd Lane's books and paintings were destroyed with his studio and Fred Bonelli lost band instruments worth £5,000, together with 5,000 musical scores and numerous costumes. The losses seriously affected Bonelli. Although under no obligation to do so, the Company offered him £500 compensation, which they later increased to £600.

The fire caused a drop in takings amounting to several thousand pounds a week. Sir Leslie announced that no permanent staff would be laid off, nor, it was hoped, any of the temporary staff. In order to replace catering facilities, some facilities were temporarily expanded and other projects brought forward. Work on a replacement Palace of Entertainment was to start in twelve months' time. The Company received help from many sources. Planning permission for new projects was rushed through by the Corporation and the Clayton Aniline Company made its staff canteen available for Children's Circus parties, etc.

One of the new projects involved converting the old animated display, housed in the original electrical installation buildings, into the Kent Restaurant. An extension was constructed to the Palm Court Restaurant and plans drawn up to extend the Lighthouse Bar and refurbish the refreshment room next to the Top Lake, both in time for Easter. Finally, as part of the alterations being undertaken at the Exhibition Hall, the old Belfast and Exhibition Hall Restaurants were rebuilt and remodelled as the Cumberland and Windermere Suites, capable of seating 250 and 700 respectively, or 1,500 if combined. The suites shared a kitchen and were provided with multi-coloured lighting effects. The walls were decorated with fifteen "photo-murals" by Syd Lane, using a special transparent pigment applied with cotton wool.

All these features were finished by the end of 1958 and the Company arranged a special spread in the Manchester Evening News to mark the opening of the new suites which, when combined, were claimed to be the largest banqueting area in the country outside London.

Work began on the new Ballroom block in the first week of 1959 and the first phase was expected to be finished by Whitsuntide, with the entire complex complete by 12th December. The contractors, Simms, Sons & Cooke, were allowed to use the Firework Island and the rear of the Firework Lake, where the old Chinese Grotto had been, as dumping grounds for rubble. The level of the island was thus raised by four feet, affording a better view of the firework displays and compensating to an extent for the loss of the firework viewing stand.

It was decided to incorporate a Wall of Fame in the new block, where star personalities could leave impressions of their hands and feet in concrete panels. Gracie Fields and Stanley Matthews were approached, and the former inaugurated the new attraction on Monday 29th June. Other personalities, including Sir John Barbirolli, Bob Hope and the footballer Pele, followed.

Progress on the new building was not as quick as expected, the contractor blaming the delay on a shortage of bricks. Although a cafeteria had opened in August, and the Edinburgh Suite in October, work was not completed until the end of February 1960. The main ballroom, the New Elizabethan, was finished in December and a Grand Charity Opening Ball was held on 17th February 1960. The BBC televised part of the event, which went out as a live broadcast entitled "Dancing through the Ages". The formal opening of the complex was performed by the Lord Mayor, Alderman Harold Quinney.

The Edinburgh Suite contained the Carlisle Lounge, the York and Crystal Bars and the Fountain Lounge. The last named featured a dancing water display activated by music. Syd Lane, now officially

The smoking ruins of the Ballroom Block on the morning of 17th January 1958

retired from Belle Vue, painted six Scottish murals for the walls of the Edinburgh Room. Fred Bonelli appeared with his Old Tyme Orchestra on Tuesdays and Thursdays, aided by Belle Vue's resident comperes, Harry and Minnie Green. More modern music was provided on other nights by Johnny Drake and his Crewmates, together with Reg Parrish on the electronic organ. Bunny Banker and his Mainstreamers appeared in the Edinburgh Suite every Saturday.

The Company was pleased with its investment, financed partly through insurance receipts, including a loss of profits claim, and maturing life assurance policies placed by the old management. Receipts were between two and three times better than the last comparable period in the old block, and the conduct of visitors had vastly improved. Catering had shown a similar growth; only fifty functions had been held in 1956, then 160 in 1957 and over 500 in 1959.

Developments in the Gardens 1958-63

The new zoological superintendent, William Wilson, at first showed a degree of enthusiasm similar to that of Gerald Iles. He provided new pictorial name boards for the cages and enclosures, drawing the animals himself, although the illustrations were considered by some to over-embellished.

Early in 1958 the first of a series of improvements was completed in the form of seven ruminant enclosures, built to a design of Gerald Iles on the western side of the Children's Zoo, and replacing a paddock laid out in 1955. The new enclosures were surrounded by a ditch, mock stone walls looking like Stonehenge and timber corrals, and contained boulders and sleeping quarters that looked like the adobe huts of Mexican Indians. The first inhabitants were Ankole cattle, zebra, oryx and llamas.

In April, work started on radical alterations to the Monkey House. Most of the cages were divided into smaller units, thereby enabling a larger number of species to be displayed. The following months saw the central pool in the Sunken Garden renamed the Square Pool Enclosure and adapted to house black-necked swans, the first time this feature was used to display animals. Plans were announced for new enclosures for pelicans, cranes and flamingos; larger quarters for camels and giraffes; new hornbill, parrot and pheasant aviaries; an animal hospital and acclimatisation house, and improvements to the aquarium and reptile house. William Wilson expressed a wish to display polar bears in an Arctic pool setting.

Other parts also saw benefits from the investments programme. New water scooters were provided on the Firework Lake, and an effigy of Diana Dors appeared in Louis Tussaud's waxworks. Work started on remodelling the Kings Hall, providing a new and larger foyer and front canopy, improved bar and cafeteria services, and a row of shops along one side, occupying quarters formerly used to house the circus elephants at Christmas. The new structures could be used for both purposes. Plans were also announced for a series of indoor tennis courts, and for a hotel overlooking safari-park-type enclosures at the Kirkmanshulme Lane and Redgate Lane corner, but neither was implemented.

In October 1958 the Kings Hall saw the holding of a Solemn High Mass in memory of the members of Manchester United Football Club killed in the Munich disaster. £342 was collected for the Lord Mayor's Munich Distress Fund.

The Gardens were still troubled by Teddy boys and in July a pitched battle involving seventy of them had to be stopped by police. Later, a party of youths was ejected from a private dance in the Cumberland Suite. In August, General Manager Jim Betts died. Three months later he was replaced by Morris Marshall, former Press, Publicity and Entertainments Manager for Morecambe and Heysham.

Longsight Station was closed to passengers in September 1958, although British Railways agreed to retain one platform for excursion traffic. This does not seem to have been used to any great extent after 1958 and rail excursions to Belle Vue had ceased altogether by the mid 1960s.

In January 1959 two Himalayan pandas died of pneumonia contracted in a notorious smog that affected the city. The old Monkey Terrace at the side of the Elephant House, disused since the remodelling of the Monkey House, was rebuilt to form a new Birdcage Walk in 1959. This concrete structure comprised a series of self-contained compartments, each with a door leading to a heated and draught-proof inner compartment. Instead of a glass or wire mesh front, the public had a view of the birds through a series of tightly-strung, horizontal fine steel wires. Zoological experts doubted the wisdom of this project and some thought the birds did not thrive well. Approval was also given for the building of a Penguinarium,

In the small enclosure adjoining the Cub's Nursery, 1950s

but this did not start for a few years. A Butchery was added to the rear of the Lion House.

Some "catacanoes" were placed on the Great Lake, where boating was now operated by a concessionaire, Mr Fisher from Ramsgate. To boost boating receipts, the Company arranged for the boundary walls around the Lake to be lowered to a height of two feet. A second landing stage was built, allowing the public to use the boats without having to gain admission to the Gardens. A windmill was erected on the island, the cost being shared equally with Mr Fisher. These modest investments were successful and boating patronage increased. The Company took advantage of the extra visitors to the lake by placing a mobile canteen next to the Hyde Road bus stop adjoining the lake.

In June 1959 several animals were stolen from the Children's Zoo, including two three-week-old rats, seven guinea pigs, a pigeon and other species. It was a foretaste of the continuous problem of vandalism that the Zoo was troubled with for the remainder of its existence.

The surroundings of the Water Chute were spruced up and work on the Kings Hall completed. This now had an extra bar, named the Fun Fair Bar, together with new seating. An ice spectacular, "Holiday on Ice", was shown for a three week period, during which the weekly wrestling shows were suspended. Another amusement arcade was laid out behind the Kings Hall and operated by the Amusement Equipment Company. Boxing, always a difficult sport to organise, had been absent from Belle Vue for many years, but moves were made to reintroduce it and a trial match was held in April. The Duke of Gloucester paid a visit to the stadium in the latter half of the year. In September, Johnnie Hoskins tried out go-karting. This ended after a few months when it was felt that the stadium was too large to create the right atmosphere for the sport. The Belle Vue ATC, which had occupied the paddock field and sports ground since the war, was persuaded to move to Company-owned land on Mount Road. The Board was considering using the sports field for more profitable purposes, but in the event it was not heavily used.

The catering stores building behind the Lion House was damaged in September, when one of the gardening staff failed to use a flame gun properly. In the same month, some straw ignited in the Elephant House whilst workmen were installing a new heating system for the Indian elephant, Ram Moti. Disaster was averted when a 17-year-old apprentice, Kevin Gill, grabbed the animal's trunk and led it to safety.

Towards the end of 1959, unhappy relations between the superintendent and the Zoo staff were causing problems for the Board. Six keepers were said to have resigned and more threatened to follow. The Board considered representations from the staff but saw no reason to act and no further resignations took place.

The Christmas Circus was televised by Granada TV; as with earlier broadcasts, ticket sales benefited and receipts were £4,000 up on the previous year.

There was another fire in January 1960, when £5,000 worth of damage was caused to a sweets kiosk and the adjoining Scooterland ride, where 24 dodgem cars were destroyed. Johnnie Hoskins left in February, to promote go-kart racing in London. At the stadium he was replaced by Ken Sharples, previously the Amusement Park manager, whilst his publicity duties were taken over by H Wilson Rogers. In March, the North's first Used Car Show was held at Belle Vue, and the following month saw the reintroduction of regular boxing matches in the Kings Hall. The shows were jointly promoted by Harry Levene and the Manchester turf accountant, Gus Demmy.

By July 1960 the rear of Firework Island had been rebuilt to form new Bear Terraces and a permanent background for the firework displays. The old Jennison bear pits were left vacant, although the Polar Bear Pit was for a time used as an outdoor lion enclosure. The new Terraces, which faced Kirkmanshulme Lane, were fronted by moats and furnished with rocks and pools; a great improvement on the old pits. A wider range of bear species could now be shown, and at one time Polar, Brown, Sun, Sloth and Asiatic bears were exhibited. The animals' sleeping quarters, provided with underfloor heating, were beneath the new backdrop for the firework displays, which resembled a castle or fort, complete with towers and gun positions. On each side of the raised display area was a castellated blockhouse, where scenery for the shows was housed. By now, the displays took place only in the autumn at 9.00pm and were regarded as a device to prolong the opening hours of the Amusement Park, especially after the Speedway meetings at 7.00pm.

Later in 1960, five enclosures for marsupials were built on land between the Bear Terraces and Kirkmanshulme Lane (formerly the rear part of the Firework Lake). These were provided with a central castellated roundhouse as sleeping quarters, and occasionally housed young lions and tigers.

In April and May the Head Keeper, Matt Kelly, went on safari to East Africa and

Inside the Sunken Garden, 1950s

brought back a collection which included giraffes, zebras, cheetahs, baboons, ostriches, oryx and a python. He was nicknamed "the White Hunter of Africa" by the rest of the Zoo staff for this and an earlier trip in the late 1940s.

On 7th April the Zoo suffered another outrageous act of vandalism when 38 birds worth about £2,000 were killed, mostly by being kicked by heavy boots. Among the dead were two swans, geese, ducks, nine penguins, two pelicans, a Chinese gander and a crowned crane. Some were found seriously injured, eggs were stolen and a store burgled. The police later apprehended three boys aged twelve, thirteen and fourteen. Bail was refused, the youths were convicted on five charges and sent to an approved school for three years. The public outcry after the massacre was so intense that the solicitor representing the accused argued that the case was being prejudiced by the emotionalism aroused in the press.

New attractions for 1960 included a flea circus, run by a "Professor" Tomlin and his wife, and a side show called Invisible Rays. Pepino and his miniature circus now featured regularly all year round and Belle Vue became a place of retirement for the circus's ageing proprietor.

Modernisation of the Longsight Hotel was proposed but not implemented, although work did start on the upgrading and extension of the Lake Hotel after the Board secured a contribution towards the cost from Hope & Anchor Breweries Ltd. Substantial alterations were also carried out to the Kent Restaurant, which was now used for private parties only. A false ceiling, a new and larger bar, larger drinking and dancing areas were provided, and the band podium was taken out of the dancing area and placed in a new single-storey extension, all at a cost of £4,250.

Cover design for Speedway programme

The 1960/61 Christmas Circus was marred when George Lockhart, the veteran ringmaster, collapsed before a matinee. His place was taken for the next few weeks by Harold Holt, equestrian director of the Blackpool Tower Circus. He shared the duties of the last night with Lockhart.

The old pumphouse behind the Camel and Giraffe House, dating from the Jennison era, was demolished in April 1961. The extensions to the Lake Hotel were finished in May, the work costing nearly £40,000. A new concert room, the Lake Room, was provided, together with the smaller Gloucester Room.

The Kings Hall was given a new sprinkler system, and on Friday 7th July "the largest bingo club in the country" opened. Britain was experiencing a series of cinema closures and their conversion to bingo halls had led to "bingo mania". Attendance at the first night was 1,710, followed by 2,000 the following week. A second weekly session was to be introduced if and when the admissions reached 3,000. This target was soon achieved and nightly attendances in September averaged 3,550, with membership increasing by 80 a day.

The Queen and Duke of Edin-

Polar bears in their enclosure, which was built in 1853. This continued in use until 1960

burgh presented the colours to the Duke of Lancaster's Own Yeomanry at Belle Vue on 24th May. The Company had those parts of the stadium and gardens on the royal route repainted and brightened up.

The management continued the improvements to the Zoo. The old Jennison firework factory between the Paddock House and the Children's Zoo, where the central pond - the original swimming baths - had been filled in two years previously, was opened out with a number of enclosures on one side, forming extensions of the indoor compartments of the Paddock House. This work cost £4,000. The Hall of Living Jewels was dismantled and the area was used to house a couple of Pere David's deer.

Later in the summer, a pheasantry was built on the Children's Zoo side of the area, at a cost of £1,500. In July, work on the Penguinarium began. In October, work started on a new extension to the Camel and Giraffe House, in a similar style to the Birdcage Walk added to the Elephant House. The new structure, which cost £7,000, replaced the old Bird of Prey Terrace, which was then in a dilapidated condition. The birds of prey were housed in a small enclosure near the Sealion House which previously housed pelicans. The Board also proposed a new enclosure for warthogs and a rebuilding of the peacock enclosure. At the same time it was felt that in order to maintain admissions, a new attraction in the form of a Great Ape House should be given serious consideration, at an estimated cost of £20,000.

In September the Board decided to terminate the contract of William Wilson, the zoological superintendent, as it was thought that he had gradually lost interest. Most of the proposals initiated since 1958 were ideas of the General Manager or the Managing Director, and were thus primarily designed to improve the Zoo's appearance, and not necessarily to further the welfare of the animals. However, in some cases the new projects achieved both purposes. It was decided that if a suitable replacement for Mr Wilson could not be found, a zoological manager should be appointed, relying on Head Keeper Matt Kelly "for practical purposes".

In November 1961 the British Transport Commission announced its intention of draining the Stockport branch of the Ashton Canal, from which the Top Lake obtained its water supply. This announcement was fortuitous because the Board had been looking for a suitable site for a bowling centre since 1959. A deal was struck with the Bernstein Brothers of Granada TV. Belle Vue would lease the Top Lake site to a new company, jointly owned by Belle Vue and Granada, and provision was made for possible further joint ventures on two adjoining areas. Work on the project did not begin until mid 1963.

The 1961/62 Christmas Circus was again televised by Granada TV. Despite its being one of the most expensive ever produced, receipts fell, owing mainly to foggy and cold weather.

The Penguinarium and new Birdcage Walk adjacent to the Camel and Giraffe House were both finished by Easter 1962. Improvements were made in the old Peacock Enclosure, now used for housing cranes. A circular structure with a thatched roof, in the style of an African rondavel, was erected in the centre. The adjacent Tree Island Pond, housing a collection of Mandarin and Carolina ducks, Bahama pintails and chiloe widgeon, was refurbished and provided with a yellow, red and black wooden structure resembling a Far Eastern Pagoda.

Early in 1962 an old toilet block at the rear of the Kent Suite was demolished, as was another block partially obstructing the entrance to the new Paddock enclosures and Pheasantry. Later that year it was decided to lay out a new rock garden, otter and mink enclosure on the site of the toilets. Also approved were plans to build a new aquarium and reptile house, expand the giraffe enclosure and convert the old Penguin House into a Small Mammal House. Since the relatively short-lived gerenuks in the mid-1950s, this building had housed cassowaries, but by 1962 was used only for storage.

The Board also gave further thought to the Great Ape House project, and to new paddocks for ostriches and emus alongside the Kirkmanshulme Lane wall next to the Paddock Range, where the inmates would be provided with log cabin shelters.

Princess Margaret attended the Gardens as Commandant-in-Chief of the St John Ambulance Brigade in July 1962. About the same time, Raymond Legge was appointed zoological superintendent. He was a past superintendent of Chester Zoo, a specialist in aquaria and latterly curator of Blackpool Tower Aquarium and Zoo. Legge was a talented artist and sculptor in wood and stone, and this led to another change in the style of the animal nameplates. These were either dispensed with completely or, for important species, replaced by rustic wooden boards bearing only the animal's name and area of origin. Like previous superintendents, he had a great love of animals, but his ideas about the presentation of species were more in tune with those of the management. Although not

The rear of the Sealion House in the late 1940s

on the Board, Legge was involved in the planning and supervision of improvements to the Zoo. A Chimps' Tea Party was introduced during July and August 1963 by the entertainer Billy Dash, who was paid £65 per week. The attraction was repeated in subsequent years.

From December 1962 the adult admission charge was increased from 2/- to 2/6d and the children's from 1/- to 1/3d. The Board asserted that these prices were still the cheapest in the country for the attractions offered.

Admissions fell during 1962, although receipts from other revenue-earning parts were increasing. Sir William Mather, the Manchester industrialist, when visiting an exhibition by helicopter in September, announced that *"there is no sophistication about Belle Vue, its car park is the gravest thing imaginable, it is out of date, has a poor image, and is located next to a slum"*. These remarks must have upset the Company, at a time when they were investing heavily to improve the appearance of the Zoo and other parts of the Gardens, and there was a spirited defence from Morris Marshall, the General Manager. Still, there was an element of truth in the criticism, although its full meaning was not appreciated for a few years.

A new Sunday dance club opened in the Elizabethan Ballroom on 18th November 1962. This was not well attended, was discontinued the following February, but was re-formed in May as a junior club known as the Top Ten Club. It was compered by disc jockey Jimmy Savile and attendances rapidly hit the 2,000 mark.

Work on improvements to the Zoo continued apace in 1963. By Easter, the new ostrich and emu paddocks had been completed, as were the otter enclosure and the extension to the giraffe enclosure. The otter enclosure comprised a natural water-worn limestone setting surrounded by a low stone wall. The extension of the giraffe enclosure involved removal of the old wooden Jolly Buffet Bar, dating from the Jennison era. Delays were encountered in the conversion of the old Penguin House to a Small Mammal House, when the building staff had difficulty in removing the old tank, which the Jennisons had obviously intended to last for some time. When complete, the old premises had been transformed so successfully that many thought it was a new building. Inside, it was divided into two sections. The first contained light and airy cages, backed by jungle foliage, to accommodate animals active in daytime, such as squirrels and coatis. The second section was for nocturnal animals such as lorises, kinkajous and tree porcupines. These were subjected to artificial daylight at night so that visitors could see them in an active state during the day.

Work started on the much-talked-about Great Ape House and Raymond Legge was authorised to purchase two gorillas and two orang-utans, which together with the chimpanzees would fill it when completed. The building was formally opened in July by comedians Morecambe and Wise. The total cost was £50,000, considerably higher than the original estimate. The unusually-designed building was provided with heating, air conditioning, humidifiers, an isolation room, kitchen and food store. The indoor compartments were viewed through thick glass windows (which tended to steam up in cold weather, hampering the public's view) and were connected by underground passages to outdoor pens, again protected from the public by armour-plated glass, for use in fine weather. Visitors walked through an open central corridor, planted with trees and rock gardens, which separated the indoor and outdoor quarters. The new attraction was well attended, but a female orang-utan died at an early date and had to be replaced by the supplier free of charge. Both chimpanzees and orang-utans successfully bred there later. The completion of the building enabled the old Cubs' Nursery building to be used for housing a family of wolves. Since the late 1950s, this had been referred to as the Small Ape House. Late in 1963 work started on the new Aquarium and Reptile House.

Other areas of the Gardens saw improvements. Refurbishment of the Palm Court Hotel was put in hand in an effort to restore poor receipts. An attraction in the Amusement Park, Dodge City, proved very popular. This was a mock gun battle in a Wild West town setting, accompanied by a running commentary. The old greenhouses adjacent to The Avenue, which had been gradually reduced in numbers over the years, were finally demolished to extend the Exhibition Hall car park. Also demolished was the old Jennison armoury, which stood in the centre of the greenhouses. New greenhouses

Circus clown Little Billy signing autographs

were erected at the Kirkmanshulme Lane/Redgate Lane corner of the Gardens.

In a search for new attractions, discussions took place with Mecca Ltd over the possibility of building an ice-skating rink, as skating was becoming very popular. The paddock field and sports ground were considered for a possible golf driving range, but they were not long enough. Towards the end of the year the Enchanted Gardens were dismantled, as the features were dilapidated and it was felt that the attraction had lost its novelty. In its place, a Veteran Car Ride was installed, the track costing £500 and the five miniature Model T Ford cars £375 each. In the Amusement Park, the Bubble Bounce was discontinued and sold. An Easter Bonnet Parade was successful, and was repeated the following year. "Professor" Tomlin's Flea Circus had to close in April when human fleas, essential for the act, could no longer be obtained. Also held for the last time was the National Scooter Rally. Started in 1961, it had then attracted 2,000 entrants, but only 300 turned up in 1963. In October, a fire destroyed the House of Nonsense and three other buildings.

Until now, Belle Vue had proved a good investment for both Sir Leslie Joseph and Charles Forte. From the dismal days of 1956, trading revenues had steadily risen to over £240,000 in 1961 and 1962, although these figures also include those for the London Festival Gardens. The dividends received by the shareholders had likewise risen to 12½% in 1958 and 50% in 1961.

Since the early 1950s the business activities of Charles Forte had expanded vastly from their milk bar origins, and it was not long before the Trust Houses Forte company was formed, following the merger with the Trust Houses hotel chain. During 1962, as part of this expansionary trend, Forte decided to "go public" and seek further capital through offering shares in his company, Fortes Holdings Ltd, on the Stock Exchange. At the same time, he decided to acquire a controlling interest in Belle Vue in order to give himself even greater management freedom, in particular over new projects involving capital investment such as the proposed joint Bowling Centre with Granada and Exhibition Hall negotiations with Manchester Corporation. It was also felt that further links between the catering side at Belle Vue and the main Forte catering organisation would be beneficial for both enterprises. In September 1962, therefore, he reached agreement with Sir Leslie for the purchase of the majority of his Belle Vue shareholding, and five months later an offer was made to the remaining small shareholders. Shares in Fortes Holdings Ltd were offered in exchange, to the value of 15/3d per Belle Vue share. By the end of the year, Belle Vue (Manchester) Ltd belonged solely to Fortes Holdings Ltd.

Sir Leslie Joseph was succeeded as Managing Director by Morris Marshall, the General Manager since 1958. Sir Leslie had put a lot of effort into the revitalisation of Belle Vue, even living on the premises for a period, and it is said that he kept a pair of overalls in his office so that he could inspect any part of the Gardens at short notice. He did not disappear from the Belle Vue scene, however; he went on to become Chairman and Managing Director of the leisure division of the Forte Holdings company and continued to conduct the negotiations with the Corporation over possible extensions to the Exhibition Halls.

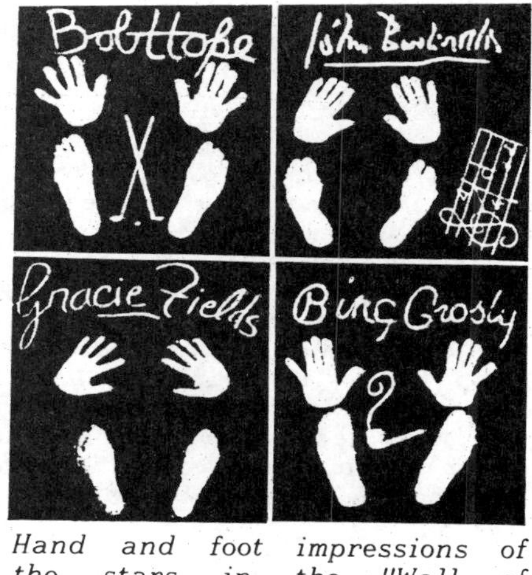

Hand and foot impressions of the stars in the "Wall of Fame", which was incorporated into the New Elizabethan Block

"Railway Queen" with its Wild West appendages in a mid-1960s publicity photograph, which itself is very much a "period piece"!

PART OF THE FORTE EMPIRE 1963-77

Developments 1963-71

The takeover by Charles Forte had little immediate effect on the development of the Gardens. The programme of improvements continued and late in 1963 work started on the Bowling Centre, following the filling in of the Top Lake. The Board decided at an early date that this should be operated separately and a high fence was erected between it and the rest of the Gardens.

By November 1963 the Kings Hall bingo sessions had begun to lose their popularity and the Friday night session ended the following March. The Sunday sessions continued until 1966.

The filling of the Top Lake had necessitated the relocation of the Miniature Railway. This now ran in an irregular circuit, 500 yards long, around the Firework Lake, passing the new Aquarium, Maze Cottage and the Marsupial Paddocks. The station was located outside the New Elizabethan, whilst the locomotives and rolling stock were housed in a concrete tunnel containing a siding near Maze Cottage, at one end of which was a model of a Mexican village. The railway was re-styled the Santa Fe Railway and the locomotives given American style features like cow catchers. The public liked the revamped attraction, for in the two weeks after its opening on 9th March, it was estimated that a quarter of the Gardens' visitors had travelled on the line.

Other schemes were put in hand to open up the area passed by the new line. Raymond Legge was asked to design new outdoor enclosures for lions and tigers. These were finished for Whitsuntide 1964 at a cost of £8,000 and were on the site of the old Jennison Bear Pits. There was a small area for Rita, the tigon, and an ingenious device for trapping the animals whenever they required veterinary attention. At the same time, the old Deer Park next to the Kirkmanshulme Lane wall was converted to a Wolf Wood, its tenants being given log cabin sleeping quarters. Since the previous year, wolves had been penned up in the old Cubs Nursery and this building continued to house a family of them until it was demolished in 1969.

The removal of the big cats to their new enclosures left the old Lion and Tiger House available for other uses. The Board considered converting it into a Dolphinarium, at a cost of £12,000, but ruled this out after it became apparent that too many dolphinaria were being established elsewhere, and that the public's demand for this type of attraction might be both limited and short lived. Two years later the old house was converted to a slot machine arcade. The adjoining aviary still housed birds, but far fewer since the building of the Birdcage Walks next to the Elephant and Camel Houses.

In mid 1964 the new Aquarium and Reptile House was finished and this was a truly outstanding building. The Aquarium had three separate halls. The first contained small tanks of tropical freshwater fish such as angels, swordtails and neon tetras, and rarer species like the pompadour, electric eels and elephant fish. The second hall was entitled "Fishes of the Coral Seas" and featured a coral reef setting with such colourful and quaintly shaped fishes as the pennant, puffer, clown, bat and lion fish. The third hall contained fish of the British lakes, rivers and coastal areas, including giant conger eels. Linking the Aquarium to the Reptile House was a special section devoted to fish which live near the water surface in search of insect food, or which come out of water, such as the climbing perch and the mud-skipper.

In the first section of the Reptile House, large and spectacular snakes and lizards were shown, each in an appropriate setting of rocky canyon, forest or desert scrub. The main hall was landscaped as a tropical forest and a waterfall flowed into a large pool. As they crossed a bridge, visitors could see crocodiles, alligators and turtles. Flying about under the glass roof were colourful small birds and the whole effect of the display was heightened when the plants were watered by sprinklers and a rainbow sometimes appeared. The final section of the Reptile House displayed small lizards and snakes, tree frogs and chameleons. It was in this section in 1972 that the Royal python was successfully bred for the first time in Europe. In the main hall, another "first" almost took place in 1965, when a pair of American alligators mated, built a nest and laid eggs, which unfortunately proved to be infertile. The whole of the new complex was served by extensive reservoirs and complicated water circulation systems behind the scenes.

Although it was an undoubted success as far as the public was concerned, the Zoo staff were less enthusiastic about the building, which was said to be difficult to work in, and some of the expensive equipment was not as perfect as it should have been. The completion of the building allowed the old open-air Reptilium near the Paddock Ranges to be put to other uses.

Fred Bonelli (right) and his orchestra with Jimmy Jewel (left) and Ben Warriss (sixth from left)

One of the locomotives of the Miniature Railway, "George the Fifth", was sold in 1964. This had lain derelict at the back of the workshops since about 1957. The locomotive was subsequently restored to working order and now operates on a line at Carnforth.

In October a serious fire destroyed the Cumberland and Windermere Suites and 3,000 people had to be evacuated from a bingo session in the Kings Hall. It took seventy firemen with fourteen appliances a full hour to get the blaze under control, and special measures had to be taken to prevent the fire spreading to diesel tanks used for the central heating system. Two firemen were injured in the blaze, which also set part of the adjoining Speedway Stadium alight. A security officer braved the encroaching flames to rescue Company documents kept in the Exhibition Hall. The main Belle Vue substation was also affected, blacking out parts of the Gardens and surrounding area for two hours. After the fire, Sir Leslie announced that the suites would be rebuilt within seven months, and in the meantime the Edinburgh Suite in the Elizabethan complex, together with temporary suites in the Lancaster Exhibition Hall, would cater for additional banqueting.

The Cumberland and Windermere Suites were rebuilt by the following September, after work had been delayed by a shortage of building materials and bad weather. The total dining area could accommodate 1,500 if the suites were combined with a new suite, the Kendal. Each had its own distinctively designed bar. The Windermere Bar had a nautical flavour, whilst the Cumberland Bar was adorned by Victorian bric-a-brac and brassware collected by Morris Marshall and Jack Fearnley from antique stalls. The Kendal Bar was in the Mexican style. Each of the new suites had its own sprung dance floor, stage and air conditioning, and could be divided from the other suites by moveable soundproofed screens.

The Bowling Centre opened early in 1965. This featured a snack bar, licensed bar, children's nursery, cloakroom, club meeting room and a 200-space car park. Each of the thirty-two lanes cost £1,800 to install, plus £4,000 for each pin setting machine. The centre was wired up to enable Granada TV to televise bowling events. A bowling craze was still sweeping the country and the centre was a success.

Firework Displays

1852 The Bombardment of Algiers
1853 The Storming of Seringapatam
1854 The Burning of Moscow
1855 The Siege of Sebastopol
1856 The Storming of Malakoff
1857 The Siege of Gibraltar
1858 The Storming of Delhi
1859 The Temple of Janus
1860 The Storming of Badajoz
1861 The Emperor's Palace and City of Pekin
1862 The Battle of the Nile
1863 The Relief of Lucknow
1864 The Siege of Charlestown
1865 The Earthquake at Lisbon
1866 Carnival of Rome
1867 The Siege of Acre
1868 The Battle of Trafalgar
1869 The Storming of Magdala
1870 The Storming of Quebec
1871 The Bombardment of Strasbourg
1872 Napoleon crossing the Alps
1873 Defeat of the Spanish Armada
1874 The Battle of Waterloo
1875 The Capture of Coomassie
1876 The Prince at Calcutta
1877 The War in Servia
1878 The Siege and Fall of Plevna
1879 The Afghan War
1880 The Burning of the Tuileries
1881 The Battle of Navarino
1882 Carnival of Venice
1883 The Battle of Tel el Kebir
1884 The Siege of Constantinople 1453
1885 The Siege and Defence of Khartoum
1886 The Storming of San Sebastian
1887 The City of London
1888 The Siege of Malta
1889 The Storming of the Bastille
1890 The Storming of Cairo
1891 The Battle of Inkerman
1892 The Battle of Cape St Vincent
1893 American Indian War
1894 The Siege of Granada/ Success to the Ship Canal
1895 The Storming of Port Arthur
1896 The Battle of Alma
1897 The Matabele War
1898 The Storming of Dargai
1899 The Soudan Campaign
1900 The Siege of Ladysmith
1901 The War in China
1902 The Battle of Paardeberg
1903 The Capture of Gibraltar
1904 The Attack on Port Arthur
1905 The Battle of Muckden
1906 Delhi during the Indian Mutiny
1907 The Battle of Blenheim
1908 The Defence of Mafeking
1909 The Bombardment of Alexandria
1910 The Battle of Manchester
1911 The Relief of Lucknow
1912 The Burning of Hankow
1913 The Balkan War
1914 The Battle of Kandahar
1915 The Battle of the Marne
1916 The War in Flanders
1917 The Battle of the Ancre
1918 The Fight for Liberty
1919 Mons 1914-1918
1920 The Capture of Jerusalem
1921 The Chinese War - the Storming of the Taku Forts
1922 The Storming of Kotah 1858
1923 The Redskins
1924 Mexico
1925 Cannibals
1926 The Reign of Terror
1927-8 Ordinary Displays
1929 The Battle of Vimy Ridge
1930 The Storming of Badajoz
1931 Waterloo
1932 China - the Sack of Pekin
1933 India - the Massacre of Cawnpore
1934 India - the Siege of Delhi
1935 Sudan - the Destiny of Egypt
1936 San Sebastian 1836
1937 The Golden Pagoda of Rangoon
1938 Fantasy Battle
1939 India 1757
1946-53 Ordinary Displays
1954 The Storming of Quebec
1955 The Relief of Lucknow
1956 Robin Hood
1957-69 Ordinary Displays

The massive programme of improvements to the Zoo now slackened off and no new projects were started in 1965. At a Roman Catholic event in the stadium that year, a message was sent to the Pope requesting the canonisation of forty English martyrs. In September it was announced that Belle Vue would accept responsibility for maintaining the National Brass Band Registry, which had been set up in 1952 to regulate the movement of players between bands. This was threatened with closure following the demise of the Daily Herald newspaper, which had run the Registry.

At the beginning of April 1966, television personality Jimmy Clitheroe opened Miniland, a model village built on part of the old paddock field and sportsground area next to the Ruminant Enclosure. Work on the models had started late in 1963, each one being made and painted by Syd Lane. The attraction was illuminated at night and contained 600 painted figures. Tableaux depicted Crofts Bank Farm, Darby and Joan, ruins of an old abbey, Ann Hathaway's Cottage, a shopping centre, Bladon in Oxfordshire, a model railway, an air terminal and a motorway leading to a "city of the future". In one corner was a Cornish fishing village, complete with quays, cottages, narrow cobbled streets, lighthouse and lifeboat station. The whole scheme cost £50,000. The old sports ground stand had to be demolished, and the rest of the sports field and paddock was advertised as a helicopter pad, although its use as such was infrequent, and it was normally used for exercising animals.

A world record was set in August 1967 by 20-year-old student Vance Sutton, who made 325 non-stop circuits on the Bobs coaster, beating the previous record of 303 circuits. In December, the dancing water displays in the New Elizabethan were replaced, at a cost of £8,000, by what was described as the largest Wurlitzer organ in Europe.

In January 1968 the veteran musician, Fred Bonelli, collapsed during a Circus matinee. He refused all offers of assistance and continued to conduct the orchestra, but an ambulance was called and he was taken to Manchester Royal Infirmary, where he died a few days later. Fred Bonelli had been, during the 1930s, 40s and early 50s, one of Belle Vue's star attractions, although his work took him to all parts of the country. His place in Belle Vue's musical affairs had diminished since the late 1950s and, apart from Circus duties, his appearances had been restricted to the Tuesday and Thursday night Old Tyme dance sessions. His place in these was taken over by Derek Butterworth.

The tigon, Rita, died of old age in February 1968. The Centenary of the Trades Union Congress was celebrated in the Kings Hall and stadium in June, the event being accompanied by brass bands. Special commemorative stamps were sold from a temporary post office near the New Elizabethan. During the 1968/69 Christmas Circus, George Lockhart, now well into his eighties, was admitted to hospital with acute pneumonia. His health had been failing for some time, and his duties in the ring had been shared with Roberto Germains and, this year, with Bobby Roberts.

Further alterations to the Lake Hotel were carried out early in 1969 to form a new bar area and an additional store room. After two years of internal debate, authorisation was given to start work on a new Tropical River House. This was one of the most ambitious projects ever undertaken, and its commencement was surprising as the Board was beginning to get alarmed at the continually falling attendances, which prompted them in August to issue instructions to keep staffing levels to a minimum. The new attraction was built as an extension to the Elephant House and necessitated demolition of the old outdoor pool and the old Cubs Nursery building. The new building cost over £60,000. In the first section was an aviary, from where visitors strolled along an elevated log causeway to view the animals. On one side were tapirs who drank at a shallow pool which was fed by a waterfall. A stream ran from here through narrow rocky walls and under the causeway into a spacious pool containing a hippo. Other species exhibited included pygmy hippos, flamingos and hornbills. Some birds flew freely, and near the exit a large compartment contained spider monkeys. Overall, the house had rather a dark appearance, and efforts to encourage plant life were not all that successful. Even some plastic foliage was eaten by the monkeys. Although the birds did not thrive particularly well, both the pygmy hippo and the Malayan tapir eventually bred. A new outdoor elephant paddock was built at the same time as the Tropical River House, covering the area where the small coypu enclosure had been.

There was another fire in September 1969. Damage, estimated at £10,000, was caused to the Ghost Train and an amusement arcade, where thirty slot machines were destroyed. 1969 was the last year for firework displays. These had gradually been losing their popularity, and unlike his predecessors, Raymond Legge was never happy with them, pointing to many cases of animals injured or dying as a result of shock. Gerald Iles, in his day, did not object to the displays, and said that for most animals they were a positive benefit, giving variety to their lives, although he admitted that the tropical fish were terrified. However, certain animals, in particular the bears, big cats and marsupials, were now much closer to the pyrotechnics and in more open enclosures than in Iles's time.

The Palm Court Hotel underwent another transformation, re-opening in September 1969 as Caesar's Palace. This now contained a bar decorated in the style of Ancient Rome. The extension erected in the 1950s was turned into a Golden Fry griddle. One casualty of these alterations was the directors' private bar, nicknamed "The Vatican". Said to have dated from the Jennison era, this panelled room had been used to entertain personalities such as the Duke of Gloucester, Churchill, Macmillan, Harold Wilson and Tommy Handley, together with "countless lords and a desert of sheiks". A new Vatican was provided for the directors, but it had none of the quality of the old one.

In 1970 the firework display area was converted, at a cost of £3,500, into a quarantine area, the first occupants in October being giraffes. The two blockhouses on each side were well suited to housing tall animals and camels were also kept there from time to time. Legislation implemented that year considerably hindered the ability of zoos to import animals, and those that could be brought in were subjected to lengthy quarantine periods. Belle Vue was well placed in this respect, for its urban location meant that the risk of transferring infectious diseases, like rabies, to other animals was slight.

H F B Iles resigned as Chairman in mid 1970, although he had played little part in the Gardens for a few years, apart from the September Brass Band Contests, where he followed in his father's footsteps. He died in 1972. The name of the Company had been changed to Entam Pleasure Parks Ltd in February and in October that company formally ceased trading. Business was thereafter

The Ghost Train in the Amusement Park, late 1940s

carried out in the name of Entam Leisure Ltd, the company which operated all the other leisure interests of Sir Charles Forte. This change of emphasis had noticeable effects on the future management of the Gardens.

Development of the Exhibition Halls 1956-71

The proposal for a large exhibition hall to serve the Manchester area was first made in 1946, when the Corporation declared that there was an urgent need for one. Neither Belle Vue, nor its competitor, the City Hall on Liverpool Road, was considered large enough. Although the Corporation listed a number of suitable sites, no progress was made until January 1951, when a site at the junction of Water Street and Quay Street was selected. Again no action followed, no doubt partly because of the need to complete post-war building commitments, although the chosen site was reaffirmed by the Council in March 1955. These proposals, not unnaturally, aroused the opposition of the Company and in October 1954 R M Dixon wrote to the Lord Mayor, expressing a formal objection to the plan and asserting that Belle Vue was quite capable of accommodating any exhibition likely to be held in the area.

Later in 1955 the Corporation agreed to release the Water Street site for the development of the Granada TV complex. At the time, it was considered that the nearby City Hall facilities were adequate and would continue in use for another eight years until required for road proposals. A replacement site for the intended exhibition hall was identified in the Strangeways area.

In 1956 the new management was fully aware of the potential for development of their Exhibition Hall, although at that time, apart from the annual round of dog shows, etc, few trade exhibitions were held because organisers were reluctant to venture away from larger London venues. The Company thought that they could attract four or five large trade shows a year. The accommodation offered by Belle Vue for the Textile Recorder Exhibition, one of the largest textile machinery exhibitions in the world, was insufficient and temporary marquees were erected as extensions each year. Then, towards the end of 1957, plans were announced for the building of two permanent extensions to the Exhibition Hall, partly financed by the organisers of the Textile Recorder event in return for concessionary letting terms in the future. This work, carried out in early 1958, produced two new 75ft-wide halls, the Lancaster and Derby Halls, on either side of the existing hall (now named the Central Hall), with floor areas of 39,700 sq ft and 24,900 sq ft respectively. The total exhibition space now amounted to 112,000 sq ft. In building the Lancaster Hall, it was necessary to remove the disused railway sidings.

The main entrance to the Palm Court Restaurant in 1968

H F B Iles, Belle Vue Chairman 1938–70

This activity coincided with renewed interest by the Corporation in building an exhibition hall, and a Bill was submitted to the 1957/58 Parliament seeking powers to develop the Strangeways site. This drew a formal objection from Belle Vue and a request that the Corporation consider either locating its hall at Belle Vue, or joining with the Company in enlarging the existing facilities. It was pointed out that Belle Vue was capable of accommodating the necessary vehicular traffic, having dealt with 2,300 cars and 105 coaches at the last Textile Recorder Exhibition. Belle Vue also had the catering facilities to satisfy the demands of visitors, being capable of supplying over 5,000 lunches in one day. As a result of this initiative, discussions began between the Corporation and Sir Leslie Joseph on behalf of the Company.

By early 1960 the City Architect had produced plans for a new 120,000 sq ft hall at Belle Vue, together with a smaller 24,000 sq ft hall, giving a total area of over 300,000 sq ft. The cost was estimated at £750,000, which the Company thought was too expensive. The Corporation revised its proposals and in September 1961 came up with a plan for a hall of 89,000 sq ft at a cost of £500,000, which they considered could be self-financing. By now, the Corporation had given up its plan to erect its own hall elsewhere, which it was advised could not be undertaken without a continuous charge on the rates.

Discussions were overtaken by events, for by late 1963 two

temporary extensions to the Lancaster and Derby Halls, the Birkenhead and Keswick Halls, had been built in asbestos by BFM Exhibitions Ltd, who had organised an annual furniture exhibition since 1959. In that year, to provide more space for the exhibition, the Company had laid a concrete base at the side of the Lancaster Hall so that marquees could be erected upon it. The cost of the work, £1,450, was recovered by renting the space to BFM, but the temporary marquees were not considered satisfactory. The new halls remained the property of BFM and were not available for letting by the Company.

In mid 1964 the Corporation revised its proposals for the exhibition hall yet again. The Company was unable to agree the terms under which the Corporation's debt charges on the new hall would be re-imbursed. The Board was now of the view that as only three exhibitions a year required a total space of 200,000 sq ft, a new hall of only 60,000 sq ft, costing £350,000, would be more appropriate. The Corporation reluctantly accepted these alterations, but the City Architect said that the size of extension now proposed was inadequate to satisfy the Corporation's original requirements and there was a danger that the Council would be financing facilities that would not be commercially attractive. It was therefore stated that the Corporation's involvement in the scheme would be conditional upon the Company modernising and adapting existing facilities in accordance with the City Architect's recommendations.

A new factor appeared in the negotiations in September 1965, when it was announced that Central Station would soon close, and the Corporation began to give consideration to its future use. One early suggestion was that it would form the ideal exhibition hall that the Corporation had been seeking, having the advantage over Belle Vue in that it was in the City Centre.

Despite this, it seemed that both parties were close to agreement by the end of 1966, for the Corporation was formally asked to ratify terms provisionally agreed. Broadly, these provided for the Council to finance and build the new 60,000 sq ft hall, which would then be equipped, managed and operated by the Company. The gross income from lettings was to be split equally, and the Company was to pay a rental on a new joint restaurant, kitchen and bar. It was over this payment that the only disagreement remained. The Corporation estimated its debt charges on this part of the accommodation to be £3,500 per annum, but the Company was only willing to offer a rent of £500 per annum, later revised to £1,750 per annum. The Corporation revised its figure to £2,500, but the Company still could not agree and negotiations broke down. The Corporation's response was to set about investigating the feasibility of converting Central Station to an exhibition hall.

This tactic had the desired effect, for early in 1967 Sir Leslie Joseph offered to increase the restaurant rent to £2,500 and discussions began again. By September 1968 the Company was once more having doubts about the size of the new hall, especially as the cost of a 60,000 sq ft hall had now risen to £500,000, and the annual running costs had risen from £21,000 to £38,000. The Company felt that the chances of attracting large exhibitions were just as good with a total capacity of 140,000 sq ft, as opposed to the 170,000 sq ft, and the Company's architects drew up such a scheme, incorporating a new entrance directly on to Redgate Lane with an attractive joint foyer and landscaping at a cost of £275,000.

Advertisement for Caesar's Palace, shortly after its conversion from the Palm Court Restaurant in 1969

In the meantime, the Company proceeded with the re-roofing of the Central Hall in early 1968, and it was also provided with a new bar. Parts of the Central and Derby Halls were combined and given an increased head-room of 40ft at its apex to enable boat shows to be held. A span of 130ft was provided with this height, the whole scheme costing £107,000.

"The Outsiders" at the "Poporama" pop group contest in the Kings Hall, 28th June 1970

The negotiations dragged on, and provisional agreement was reached in early 1970. The Corporation was to build the new hall within three years on land leased from the Company, and lease the hall back to the Company for 99 years. The Company was to equip and run the hall, the gross receipts being divided according to the share of the capital contributed by each party.

This agreement came too late, for in May 1970 the Conservatives were displaced by Labour in the municipal elections. The Labour Party had always been sympathetic to the Central Station plans and they were also against concentrating all the city's exhibition facilities in one location at Belle Vue. The Company made one final approach the following year, when it was stated that it had received an offer to purchase part of the site. Despite a meeting between Sir Leslie Joseph and the Council leader, Sir Robert Thomas, no further interest was shown by the Corporation.

Years of Decline 1971-77

Attendances fell throughout the later 1960s, the years 1968, 1969 and 1970 being particularly disastrous. From an average Easter Bank Holiday Monday gate of over 150,000 in the early 1960s, admissions on such days had now dropped to around 30,000. The Company was forced to take action, putting the operation of each part of the Gardens under continuous review, with the aim of keeping costs to a minimum and dispensing with those attractions which were no longer felt to be profitable. The last Railway Carnival was held in 1970, as its attraction had declined to a point where the Company lost money on the venture. With decreasing attendances, many features of the Gardens had already disappeared. Pepino's Circus, the fireworks displays and Dodge City were all no more, and the Vintage Car ride in the Enchanted Garden area was replaced by a set of dinosaurs.

The Amusement Park, too, had begun to contract slowly, and the Tumblebug and Caterpillar rides were discontinued around this time. Of the Company-operated rides, which now only amounted to about half of the Amusement Park, most were over ten years old. The proportion of the Amusement Park operated by concessionaires steadily increased, one of the more prominent operators being Alf Wadbrooke, who had first appeared at Belle Vue in the 1950s. The hours of opening of the Amusement Park were gradually reduced and restricted to weekends only after the end of the summer school holidays. By now all animal rides, with the exception of pony rides, had ended. Elephant rides, in particular, were felt to be potentially dangerous and did not accord with current thinking on animal welfare.

The Miniature Railway also showed signs of decline, although it lost its North American features and was renamed the Belle Vue Steam Railway by the end of 1971. After 1971, rarely more than one locomotive was in service at any one time, but an additional locomotive, "Joan", had been transferred to Belle Vue following the closure of the Rhyl Miniature Railway in 1969 by an associated company in the Forte group.

A small exhibition of Belle Vue memorabilia, which had been started a few years earlier with the intention of forming a museum, was closed and the exhibits literally thrown away.

All these negative changes proved part of a vicious circle; with fewer attractions, there were fewer visitors to Belle Vue. The catering business, so important to Forte's original interest in Belle Vue, had also shown signs of decline. After reaching a peak in the early 1960s, the Company found it had to strive hard to fend off competition from hotels in the leafy South Manchester and Cheshire suburbs which were cashing in on the trade. Belle Vue had to respond by keeping charges down, and the total catering receipts in 1970 were little different from 1965, despite a period of inflation in the meantime. In the New Elizabethan complex, nightly dancing continued, but the attendances on Friday and Saturday nights suffered a drastic drop in 1969 and 1970, and continued to fall thereafter. The Top Ten Club, which only four years earlier had been billed as the "largest teenage dance club in the country", lost the services of Jimmy Savile in 1968 and struggled on to close in 1970.

The Zoo was experiencing difficulties, although the animal collection was still impressive in its breadth of species, and was still at the forefront when it came to standards of care for its inmates. David Taylor, the Zoo's vet, had pioneered many innovations in veterinary care since the early 1960s. The breeding record continued to be exemplary, exceeding many of the country's non-commercial zoos. The Zoo's ability to acquire animals was seriously hampered both by financial restrictions and by the recently introduced quarantine regulations. However, under an arrangement with a Salford-based animal importer, animals destined for other collections were kept in the newly formed quarantine enclosure and this provided additional income. The Company sought to extend this facility and parts of the Paddock House were later put to the same use.

Although it is difficult to identify any specific cause, the Zoo and the rest of Belle Vue had begun to appear very dated and unsophisticated at

The locomotive "Joan" and train, with the New Elizabethan and the Water Chute in the background, about 1974

the start of the 1970s. Despite the improvements, it was still regarded as an old fashioned urban zoo, the style of which was being rapidly eclipsed by the new generation of safari and wildlife parks. An increasingly hard-to-please public was also unlikely to find Belle Vue's dated and comparatively unkempt buildings an attractive setting for a day out. The management was not unaware of this, but its exhortations to staff to adopt a tidier approach were not all that successful. In any event, the appearance of Belle Vue could only get worse, as after 1970 building maintenance was restricted to emergency work only, and the Works Department lost some two-thirds of its staff complement of about thirty as part of the general reductions in staffing levels imposed by the management after 1969.

Particularly harmful from the commercial point of view was the opening of Knowsley Safari Park in 1971 and the new municipal zoo at Blackpool in 1973. Rather than counter these competing attractions directly, Belle Vue seemed to play down the importance of the Zoo in its advertising, and concentrated on the Amusement Park instead. Many felt this apparent change to be misguided, as over 60% of visitors until then had come because of the Zoo, patronising the other attractions as a spin-off for Belle Vue. On the other hand, many measures had been adopted to increase animal welfare in the Zoo, such as prohibiting the public from feeding the animals. The overall policy of the Zoo, however, remained as it had always been - to display as broad a spectrum of species as was possible. Some zoological authorities argue that this was a mistake and that Belle Vue should have concentrated on displaying those elements best suited to city zoos. However, the financial pressures were such that no changes involving substantial capital expenditure could expect to receive Board approval.

The start of the 1970s saw a marked change in management style, following the absorption into the Entam Leisure organisation. More decisions were taken at national or regional level and the degree of autonomy allowed to Belle Vue was reduced. After 1971, the post of Managing Director was abolished and responsibility for day-to-day management left with the General Manager. Some of the General Managers installed by Entam after 1971 were widely felt to lack the keen interest and enthusiasm for the job that Morris Marshall had shown, and which would be needed more than ever if Belle Vue were to respond effectively to the challenges it would face.

The Company's profit after tax was only £49,981 for the nine months ending in October 1970, the last period in which separate accounts were produced. This compared with £81,967 for 1961/62. Also, the 1970 figure included profits earned at the Golden Garter Theatre Club in Wythenshawe, which had been opened by Belle Vue in 1968. (The figures no longer included those for the Festival Gardens.)

Yet it was not all gloom and it would be wrong to conclude that Trust Houses Forte had lost interest in the site. Wrestling, Speedway and the Circus continued to attract crowds and the exhibition halls were doing well. The Brass Band contests, after undergoing a gradual decline, enjoyed a revival in the early 1970s with the significant upturn of interest in brass bands. The Kings Hall was also filled to capacity on many occasions in the early 1970s as a venue for Rock and Pop concerts, and in 1971 the Hall saw the first match in the England v China table tennis series that marked the thawing of diplomatic relations between China and the West.

One of Belle Vue's most important landmarks, the Bobs Coaster, was demolished at the start of 1971. Maintenance costs were considered excessive and there was no longer a demand for two gravity rides in the Amusement Park. At the time, the Bobs was still being listed in the Guinness Book of Records as the world's fastest gravity ride, capable of speeds in the region of 61mph. The structure

Advertisements from a 1971 programme

was sold to an Oldham demolition contractor who agreed to sell small parts of it to souvenir hunters. The removal of the Bobs gave the management the opportunity to open up a more direct line of approach to the Kings Hall from the Hyde Road entrance.

In December 1971 Trust Houses Forte offered to sell the Zoo to Manchester Corporation as a going concern. However, the Corporation was interested in the site for municipal housing and the Company was not willing to sell on this basis.

In the same month, Raymond Legge resigned and left to manage a drive-in wildlife park in Spain. He was succeeded by Peter Grayson, a Manchester man, who had earlier held posts at Flamingoland in Yorkshire and who had been Legge's deputy for the previous three months. The fact that the Zoo still had an excellent reputation zoologically was reflected in January 1972 when seven Barbary apes were presented by the Officer-in-Charge of Gibraltar, where there was a population problem among the Rock's inmates. Two of the species had been sent ten years earlier in similar circumstances and one of their offspring still survived. The entire collection was placed in the Gibbon Cage.

Proposals were made in 1972 to use the Sealion House for dolphin displays, coinciding with the venture by the Entam company into running dolphinaria at Knowsley and Woburn. Sir Leslie Joseph was keen that Belle Vue should hold some dolphins in reserve for use elsewhere. As an experiment, a trial show was arranged in a marquee on the Hyde Road car park. Despite the success of this, the show in the Sealion House did not materialise. Peter Grayson was opposed to the plan; the pool was far too shallow and lacked the necessary technical facilities, such as a water purification plant.

A new attraction was introduced in 1972 behind the Kings Hall in place of the Electric Speedway ride. Named Rolarena, it consisted of a roller skating rink, again operated by a concessionaire.

The Christmas Circus for 1972/73 was the first that did not feature George Lockhart, who had finally retired from the ring at the age of ninety. Like Fred Bonelli, Lockhart was a name always associated with Belle Vue. He had enjoyed a long career in the circus and had first stepped into the ring at the age of six, playing the

George Lockhart, Belle Vue's famous Ringmaster

part of Prince Charming in a circus in Sweden. He had appeared in revue, films and on the stage, but the circus was his first love. As a ringmaster, he had complete authority over the shows and their various acts, yet he was able to charm and entertain the audiences. George Lockhart's place at the Belle Vue Circus was taken for the next two years by Danish-born "Nelly Jane", Belle Vue's first woman ringmaster.

By 1973 the public's attraction to Ten Pin Bowling had decreased to the extent that the joint Belle Vue/Granada company, Belle Vue Bowling Centre Ltd, applied to convert the building into a bingo hall and social club. The magistrates turned down the application.

Quite a few improvements were undertaken in 1973/74 in an effort to capitalise on various entertainment fashions. In the New Elizabethan complex, by now collectively advertised as Danceland, the Fountain Lounge was converted to an amusement centre, capable of running prize bingo on a small scale. Also, at a cost of about £6,000, the Crystal Room was converted to the Zoo-be-Doo discotheque. The Bavarian Restaurant, no longer needed for catering, became the Bavarian Beer Halle and the reopening ceremony was performed by the Coronation Street Star, Doris Speed. Music was provided by a German-style "oompah band". An attempt was made to revive the Top Ten Club as the Stardisc Club. This started off in the revamped Bavaria building, later transferring to the Zoo-be-Doo disco.

Elsewhere, the cutbacks in expenditure had begun to give the Gardens a dilapidated look. Six students from Didsbury College of Education, who were to take a party of children to the Zoo, cancelled the trip after seeing the poor state of some of the enclosures. Later, they wrote to the press about "this disgusting heartless side-show" and pointed out that it was possible for children to touch the animals in Wolf Wood and in the Big Cats enclosures.

In 1974 the Monkeyrama display in the Amusement Park was discontinued. It had long been felt that this was an inappropriate place for the animals in view of the adjacent distractions, especially at night. However, the troupe of baboons which was finally removed from there was found to be in a near perfect condition.

The 1975 Brass Band Contest was the best attended since 1947, but there was uproar when the test piece, "Fireworks" by Elgar Howarth, was performed. There were shouts of "Rubbish!" when the judges, including Howarth, filed out after the contest. The piece has since become accepted in Brass Band circles and is widely played.

The Scenic Railway closed in 1975 after it had been decided that the cost of repairs was uneconomic. About this time, the Zoo was finally separated from the Amusement Park by a high fence, replacing a fence erected at the instigation of Raymond Legge in the 1960s, which had allowed the Zoo to be closed off at night. The new fence was designed to allow entry to the Amusement Park at nominal admission charges.

Matt Kelly, the Zoo's Head Keeper, retired in 1975 at the age of 65. For some time he had been suffering from a rare disease contracted through working with parrots, which left him with a collapsed lung. He continued to be seen around the Gardens, however. George Wilbourne, who had taken over in the Sealion House some years earlier, also retired in poor health, to be replaced by "Captain" Burgess.

Caesar's Palace, at the Hyde Road entrance, was converted to Jennison's Ale House in 1976. The Golden Fry griddle at the rear became another amusement arcade. In May, the animal broadcaster Johnnie Morris visited the Zoo. After speaking to an audience of 3,000 children in the Kings Hall, he took a walk through the Gardens accompanied by a baby chimp named Topaz. The previous month had seen one of the rare strikes by the Gardens' work-force. Ostensibly this was over a move by the management to get some of the cleaning staff to carry out new duties, and also over an employee involved in irregularities concerning the purchase of confectionery. Another strike, this time for forty-eight hours, occurred in May, when most of the Zoo staff walked out in protest at the sacking of four women cleaners from the Kings Hall who had refused to clean other accommodation. On this occasion, Peter Grayson had to feed the animals, helped only by Topaz the chimpanzee. Three volunteers came forward to assist with the cleaning of some of the cages and enclosures but some had to be left not cleaned. These staffing difficulties were only symptoms of the general financial problems, as even more stringent economies were introduced by the local management to cut costs further.

Despite this, the years 1975, 1976 and 1977 saw better attendances, partly owing to good weather and the improved quality of the collection. By this time a small riding school had been established by Peter Grayson and his wife, both keen riders, on the lawn next to the Great Ape House. Pony rides were also organised here, although by 1976 these had transferred to the Quarantine Enclosures when the quarantine service was brought to an end.

Belle Vue's economic position continued to worsen. Particularly distressing was the large rise in oil prices after 1974, as most of the heating installations were oil-fired. Many of the indoor houses, especially the older structures, became extremely expensive to run and this, together with the ever increasing cost of animal foodstuffs, meant that losses on the Zoo were running at unacceptable levels. Advertising had been drastically cut back, thus reducing the chances of attracting back the crowds who were spending their leisure time abroad or in the increasing number of country parks then being promoted by local authorities. Belle Vue Zoo Park seemed to have no place in the new order of things.

The Zoo's losses could no longer be offset by profits from other areas of the Gardens, for in the main these too were now declining seriously. Ballroom dancing had virtually finished, catering was in decline and the number of Pop concerts held in the Kings Hall had dwindled following the conversion of the old ABC Cinema at Ardwick into the Apollo Theatre. A fire destroyed the Kent Restaurant in 1976 and the Gorton Philharmonic Society transferred their concerts to Stockport that year. Only the traditional stalwarts of Wrestling, Speedway, the Circus and the Exhibition Hall were healthy, the last named benefiting from the final closure of the City Hall in 1976.

Closure of the Zoo 1977-79

At 10.00am on 4th August 1977 it was announced on BBC Radio that the Zoo would close on 11th September, at the end of the school holidays. The staff of 24 keepers had been informed of the news one hour earlier. The Company stated that it could no longer afford to contain the losses being incurred on the Zoo, said to be running at around £100,000 a year. Apart from the high heating costs and the fact that many of the older buildings had reached the end of their useful life, especially after a period of low maintenance levels, the cost of animal foodstuffs had recently escalated, amounting to £4 per animal per day, rising to £7 a day for animals like the chimps and orang-utans which required specially imported foods.

The animals were to be sold for an estimated £100,000. Many were regarded as good breeding stock, especially the orang-utans, which had recently bred, the Malayan tapir and the rare pygmy hippo. The public would be allowed to buy some of the fish and birds. Peter Grayson and the staff would all be offered jobs elsewhere.

At the end of August the Zoo suffered one of its final acts of vandalism when a number of non-poisonous reptiles was stolen from the Reptile House. One ten-foot-long python was later found in the foliage nearby, but the theft was felt to be a "professional job".

Public reaction to the closure was comparatively muted. Attendances in the final few weeks were slightly up, but even on the final day, no crowds appeared. Efforts were made to save the Zoo or form a mini zoo elsewhere, and Peter Grayson tried to establish a zoological society, hoping for sponsorship from local companies, education authorities and the Greater Manchester Council. However, the financial resources to rescue the Zoo or to start it elsewhere could not be marshalled in time. In fact, after the official closure on 11th September the gates remained open until early November, the public continuing to be admitted at reduced charges as animals were sold. Gradually the staff were laid off, most of them refusing offers of non-zoo work made by the Company.

The sale of the zoological collection was a long and drawn out affair. Many enquiries from the public had to be rejected as the animals in question were unsuitable for domestic confinement. The Zoo's colony of domestic cats, which had numbered over a hundred in Gerald Iles's day, found homes through the departing keepers. Negotiations for the larger animals were handled by Peter Grayson, who almost succeeded in raising the amount he originally

The Longsight Entrance in the early 1970s. The original Ballroom above this entrance was demolished in the mid-1950s

estimated as the sale value. Twiggy, one of the elephants, aged nine and recently arrived in the Zoo from Glasgow, went to a zoo at Amersfoort in the Netherlands. Madrid Zoo acquired four alligators. The tigers went to Tokyo Zoo and the orang-utans were bought by the manager of the pop star, Tom Jones. Nick and Babs, two Capuchin monkeys, were taken to the small zoo at Knaresborough, and some of the chimps were bought by a travelling circus. Blanco and Levi, two young lions, were bought by Robert Fossett, the lion trainer who had featured in the Circus for a number of years. Two red deer went to a zoo in the South of England, and Lucy and Shandy, two Shetland ponies, found a home on a farm at Denshaw, having been bought by a girl who had been an assistant keeper.

The fate of some of the other animals was not so good. The hippo Hercules, a favourite inhabitant of the Tropical River House, went to Cleethorpes Zoo, which closed shortly after his arrival. He was then acquired by Dudley Zoo, where he died shortly afterwards. Bristol Zoo had purchased Thomas the tapir, Dot, another hippo, and one of the gorillas, Susie. Her mate, Jo Jo, went to Chester where, despite apparent good health at Belle Vue, he fell ill and died, no doubt partly because of his enforced separation from his companion. Some of the bears and dingos were put down in early 1978, as it was impossible to give them away to people capable of looking after them properly. Peter Grayson took on the unenviable task himself.

To cut down on rates and maintenance liabilities and pave the way for the ultimate sale of the site, some of the old Zoo buildings, notably the old Pepino's Circus structure and the Aquarium and Reptile House, were demolished, the latter after some of the remaining stock had escaped one night. Other buildings were vacated and virtually abandoned, not even being cleared of the detritus left by their last tenants.

In 1978 there were still sufficient animals in the Zoo's collection to be exhibited as a Pet's Corner in some enclosures between the Kings Hall and the Elephant House. Shown here were bear cubs, macaws, Nubian goat kids, gibbons, lambs, calves, a pony, rabbits and ornamental bantams. Ellie May, a 15-year-old elephant, was also on show. At the time no suitable purchaser could be found for her, partly because she had wrongly acquired a reputation for being a dangerous animal, having been confused with the Zoo's other elephant, Twiggy. Peter Grayson had resolutely refused to see the animal killed as he felt that it was only a matter of time before a home could be found, but the expense of feeding was becoming a cause for concern. Peter Grayson left the Zoo in January 1979, but kept returning to oversee Ellie May, by then the only animal remaining. The following month Rotterdam Zoo agreed to take her, but when it was time to move her the unfortunate animal refused to complete the ascent up the ramp and into her transport. In fact, she refused to move at all and sat down. Pneumonia and heart failure set in overnight and the next morning neither Peter Grayson nor David Taylor thought the animal could be saved. A marksman was sent for to put her out of her misery.

It seemed a sad and inappropriate end for a zoo which had been in existence for over 140 years.

1977 TO THE PRESENT DAY

The Final Years under Trust Houses Forte 1977-81

When closure of the Zoo was announced, the Company declared that the remaining facilities were to be expanded with "new active leisure pursuits", and as a sign of this, the 1978 season operated under the description, "Belle Vue Leisure Park". A skateboard arena was laid out in the Tropical River House to cater for a craze then popular with youngsters. This closed after only a few months and the arena was relaid outside the New Elizabethan, by which time demand for the facility had virtually ended. Also operated that year was the Jetstream ride in the Amusement Park, which had been installed the previous year after removal from Battersea on closure of the London Festival Gardens. Despite an announcement in the press that the veteran ride was to be restored to working order, the Scenic Railway did not operate.

Other features closed in 1977, particularly those located in the Zoo area. There was no more boating on Firework Lake, and the Lighthouse Bar and Miniland were discontinued. So, too, was the Miniature Railway, where the locomotive "Joan" was leased to the enthusiast Sir William McAlpine. The other locomotives were taken to Rhyl for storage. Shortly afterwards, Sir Charles Forte was persuaded to present "Prince Charles", unused since 1971, to the Eskdale (Cumbria) Trust, which restored the engine to its former glory as "Synolda", its original name. The locomotive is now kept at the railway museum at Ravenglass and occasionally sees action on the Ravenglass and Eskdale Railway.

Facilities were run down or discontinued. The Bavaria featured Hans Becker's Original Oompah Band on only three nights a week, and there were weekly celebrity appearances in the New Elizabethan, together with the Zoo-be-Doo discotheque, although ballroom dancing had ended for good. Neither building reopened in 1979, except for the occasional private function in the Bavaria.

In 1978 Trust Houses Forte engaged a firm of planning consultants to carry out an appraisal and seek the views of the local planning authority as to what types of development would be favourably considered. In spite of this, the Company would have been in no hurry to sell the site, or even part of it; in 1975 the Labour Government had introduced legislation which effectively prevented owners from recovering much of the development value accruing from such sales.

For 1979 the Amusement Park was leased in its entirety to the main concessionaire, Alf Wadbrooke, who ran it at weekends during the season. The Scenic Railway remained out of action and the Water Chute operated for a short time before it too fell silent. Events continued as normal in the Kings Hall and the Exhibition Halls. To ease the eventual disposal of the site, Trust Houses Forte bought out the interest of BFM Exhibitions Ltd in the Birkenhead and Keswick Halls. 1979 also saw the death, at the age of 97, of veteran ringmaster George Lockhart.

The election of a Conservative Government in 1979 led to the repeal of the legislation which would have discouraged the Company from disposing of the site, and the way was clear for final closure. It became apparent that the best course of action was to sell the entire site, for those elements that remained profitable were insufficient to justify continued operation of Belle Vue as a single entity. By 1980, discussions with the City Planners had resulted in broad agreement that a mixture of housing and industry would be appropriate for the site, and early in the year, part of the Belle Vue Street car park was sold for a housing association development. On the main site, the maintenance staff was further reduced by voluntary redundancies and the Catering Department, whose activities were now almost wholly restricted to the Cumberland, Windermere and Kendal Suites, was amalgamated with the Exhibition Hall for operational purposes.

On 15th August 1980 the front parapet of Jennison's Ale House fell on to the forecourt. An emergency survey revealed that the building was in bad condition, and the Ale House and the adjoining Advance Booking Office closed the next day. The building also contained what remained of the offices used by the Company's local management; they moved from the first floor to the old Golden Fry restaurant area, which was safer. Eventually, at a cost of

Belle Vue Officials

CHAIRMEN OF BELLE VUE (MANCHESTER) Ltd:

1925-28 Sir William Gentle
1928-37 J H Iles
1938-70 H F B Iles

GENERAL MANAGERS:

1925-41 George Wilson
1956-58 J W Betts
1958-64 W M Marshall
1966-73 J F Fearnley
1974-76 C Hind
1976-78 C King
1978 I Brown
1978-79 A Coppin
1979-81 A Lee

PUBLICITY MANAGERS:

1932-38 W Rubenstein
1938-45 P F Chandhor
1945-56 D Buckland-Smith
1956-60 J Hoskins
1960-64 H Wilson Rogers
1964-81 Norman Roland*

ZOOLOGICAL SUPERINTENDENTS:

1925 George Jennison
1933-57 G T Iles
1957-61 W Wilson
1962-71 R Legge
1971-78 P Grayson

HEAD KEEPERS:

1946-75 Matt Kelly
1975-77 John Christy

HORTICULTURAL SUPERINTENDENTS:

Leslie Cook
J B Brook

MANAGING DIRECTORS:

1925-37 J H Iles
1938-41 George Wilson
1941-47 E O Spence
1947-56 R M Dixon
1956-62 Sir Leslie Joseph
1962-65 W M Marshall (later Deputy Chairman)
1965-71 K Paxton

SCENIC ARTISTS:

1852-94 George Danson & Sons
1894-96 Messrs Caney & Perkins
1896-1912 R Caney
1912-17 B Hastain & R Caney
1918 Charles Caney
1919-22 B Hastain & C Caney
1923-33 B Hastain
1935-39 O Simpson
1947-68 Syd Lane**

SPEEDWAY MANAGERS:

1929-41 E O Spence
1941-52 A S Hart
1953-60 J Hoskins
1960-63 K Sharples
1964-65 H Jackson
1966-72 Dent Oliver
1972-73 Frank Varey
1974-81 Eric Boocock

WORKS MANAGERS:

1925-44 C Wiseman
W Ray
F Jenkinson
F Selby

* Employed as adviser only.
** Retained on freelance basis only after 1957.

over £12,000, the front of the building was demolished and the remainder suitably adapted and made good. The work was finished by March 1981.

Mr Wadbrooke was given notice to terminate operation of the Amusement Park by 26th October 1980, and to remove all his equipment by the following February. Also closed that month was the Belle Vue Smithy, located behind the old Aviary, a relic of the Jennison era. It contained a complete 200-piece tool set, which was later sold. The smithy had seen little use since the Zoo's closure in 1977.

Sale of the Gardens 1981 - 82

In January 1981 it was announced that most of the main site was to be sold to the Espley Tyas Development Group in a £2.2 million deal. Trust House Forte was to retain the Speedway Stadium, Bowling Centre and Lake Hotel, and be responsible for honouring all contractual commitments in the Kings Hall to the end of the 1981/82 Christmas Circus. Espley Tyas, a recently established Birmingham based development company, would similarly honour all contracts for the exhibition halls for eighteen months following completion of the sale. The deal was conditional upon planning permission for the desired range of uses being granted before 14th July. The application submitted by Espley Tyas included a 20-acre residential area adjoining Kirkmanshulme Lane, 22 acres of industry, a major retail store and a large leisure complex consisting of a night club, discotheque, studio cinemas, bingo hall, health centre, 14 squash courts, public house, bank, toyshop, travel agent's, betting office and parking for 850 cars. The exhibition halls would be retained and refurbished. The proposals, in March, were welcomed by the City Council.

Rumours that the exhibition halls were to be demolished led to the formation of a Belle Vue Exhibitions Action Committee and representations were made to the City Council by 23 promoters. The promoters of the Rod and Custom Car Show decided to take more positive action, formed a development group called Sharilheath and in July announced a rebirth plan to reopen Belle Vue as a type of Disneyland, incorporating a Zoo, the Kings Hall and other remaining features. The proposals were supported by the North West Tourist Board, the Victorian Society, the Manchester Chamber of Commerce and the newly formed Zoological Society of Greater Manchester. A Belle Vue Action Group was also formed, which set about organising a petition to the City Council objecting to the Espley Tyas scheme. Ten thousand signatures were obtained in the first week and another five thousand the following week. Faced with these objections, the City Council deferred the granting of planning permission until August.

The matter did not rest there, for no sooner had the major application been granted than a separate detailed application was submitted by Wimpey, the housebuilders, relating to a large part of the residential sector of the site that they agreed to buy from Espley Tyas. A move to defer consideration of this application by the Planning Committee "to allow public consultation" was lost by nine votes to four, but the Greater Manchester Council ordered the City Council to defer the matter for one month. Several City Councillors commented on the size and strength of the public outcry, drawing comparisons with the relatively muted reaction to the earlier closure of the Zoo. The Action Group's petition, now containing some twenty thousand signatures, was handed to the Lord Mayor by a delegation including Matt Kelly, the Zoo's former Head Keeper. The objectors declared that they were willing to consider any scheme for the future that retained Belle Vue as a place of entertainment.

Towards the end of the month a telegram was sent to the Secretary of State for the Environment, Michael Heseltine, demanding that he exercise his powers to "call in" the application. This he would not do, and the application, for 397 houses, flats and bungalows, was granted in October. The Action Group reacted by referring the City Council's conduct of the matter to the Local Government Ombudsman. They also wrote to the area's Members of Parliament and enlisted the support of the Manchester Federation of Community Associations and such diverse personalities as Tony Benn, Joan Bakewell, Dave Lee Travis and Jimmy Savile. By October, the petition included fifty thousand signatures.

All this was in vain, for the sale to Espley Tyas finally took place in September and Sharilheath had withdrawn its own planning application in August. Wimpey and Espley Tyas set to work demolishing most of the remaining buildings, including the New Elizabethan complex, although Wimpey salvaged the Wall of Fame. A spine road (Scarcroft Road), linking Hyde Road to Kirkmanshulme Lane, was constructed, together with a new sewerage system to serve the entire site.

Final Events in the Kings Hall

Trust House Forte continued to run the Kings Hall until the end of the 1981/82 Circus. The

The rear of the old main entrance, which was being used as the Advance Booking Office by 1968 and was demolished in 1980

final, tearful Brass Band Contest was held in September and the work of the National Brass Band Registry was taken over by two local enthusiasts, supported financially by Harry Mortimer, who had virtually run the last two contests. On 2nd November the last Festival of Remembrance was arranged by the Royal British Legion and at the end of the month the final wrestling match was held. This was attended by Jack Pye, a 78-year-old star of the game who had appeared at Belle Vue until he was in his sixties.

The 53rd and final Circus opened on 26th December and featured Martin Lacey's lions, two of which had been born in the Zoo, Robert Fossett's performing elephants, footballing dogs and performing sealions, the Garcia Troupe (acrobats from Spain), the Four Brizios (the world's worst decorators) and leading clown Jacko Fossett, who had been with the Circus for over thirty years. The ringmaster was Norman Barratt.

Early in February 1982 Espley Tyas agreed to delay demolition of the Kings Hall by two weeks to allow the North West Amateur Brass Band Championships to take place. There had been a fire at Bolton Town Hall, the planned venue, and a new location had to be found quickly. Fifty-six bands took part and the winners were the Dobcross Band, while the Lostock Hall Memorial Band made their first and last appearance at Belle Vue. At the conclusion, the Glossop School Band played "Auld Lang Syne". It was a fitting end for the building.

Development of the Site since 1982

In March 1982 Trust House Forte sold the Speedway Stadium, together with part of the Redgate Lane car park, to Stuart Bamforth, the head of a group of demolition and development companies, in a transaction said to be worth in the region of £400,000. Bamforth was also a speedway and stock car promoter and he had won the 1976 World Stock Car Title at the White City, Stretford.

At an early date Bamforth announced a series of improvements. The track was widened and brought up to international standards; new floodlights and a bar and restaurant close to the Hyde Road entrance were built, and the 1982 Overseas Individual World Speedway Championship was held at Belle Vue. During this period, the use of the Stadium was virtually restricted to the Saturday night Speedway meetings and about nine Stock Car events a year. Bamforth sought other uses for the remaining nights of the week, encountering the same problems that John Henry Iles had faced in the early 1930s. A series of horse events was tried and in 1984 the Manchester Spartans American Football team used the Stadium, before transferring to the nearby Greyhound Stadium. Mr Bamforth also proposed to introduce the American sport of tractor pulling, but this did not materialise.

Harry Mortimer, famous Brass Band conductor and adjudicator. He was responsible for securing the continuance of the September Brass Band Contest in its last years at Belle Vue, and thereafter at the Free Trade Hall

Trust House Forte sold the Lake Hotel to the Burtonwood Brewery Co in 1982. They redecorated the building, ran it for a few years, then closed it in the late 1980s. The property is currently (mid 1991) derelict and is being offered for sale. Part of the Redgate Lane car park, including the three Belle Vue Place houses, was sold to British Rail in the mid 1980s for an extension to the Longsight locomotive depot. The remaining Company-owned houses on Norman Street were sold to the sitting tenants and the housebuilders, Bellway, later bought part of the Kirkmanshulme House site, after attempts to market it for industrial use had failed. The remainder of that site was developed by the Jehovah's Witnesses as a Kingdom Hall. The remaining part of the Redgate Lane car park was eventually bought by the City Council for the construction of part of the Intermediate Ring Road, which opened between Longsight and Hyde Road in 1990.

Only the Bowling Centre site remained in Company ownership and this, together with all the other leisure interests of Trust House Forte, was sold to the First Leisure Corporation, a company controlled by Lord Delfont which owns the Tower and the three piers at Blackpool, in a £37.5 million deal completed in mid 1983. Trust House Forte retains a substantial shareholding in the Company. The Bowling Centre itself, jointly operated with the Granada company, has undergone a revival of fortune in recent years and is now the GX Superbowl. A snooker club, Breaks, was built in 1985 on part of the Bowling Centre car park.

Wimpey, in the meantime, had been pressing on with their part of the site and in April 1982 the showhouse was opened by Coronation Street star Johnnie Briggs. As a mark of respect for the history of the site, roads on the new estate were named after Johnnie Hoskins and George Lockhart, although some regretted that the Jennisons appeared to have been forgotten. Sales of houses on the estate were slow and development was halted. The Ombudsman finally cleared the City Council of maladministration by May 1982, but the decision was irrelevant as the opposition had by then melted away. Wimpey had made arrangements to preserve certain groups of trees on the site and entered into an agreement with the City Council for their maintenance after completion of the estate.

Signs on the Wimpey estate

On the rest of the site, Espley Tyas demolished the remaining buildings and the Kings Hall, although the Far Eastern Pagoda, the Round House and Miniland remained until 1985. The Longsight Hotel continued to operate, being still the venue for that august body of aquarists, the Belle Vue Aquarium Socety, founded by Gerald Iles in 1936. Also still operating were the Exhibition Halls and adjoining suites. Nine of the Belle Vue staff, including Dick Talbot, had been taken on by Espley Tyas to administer these. The suites were subsequently let to a concessionaire, General Catering Services of Salford, who made some attempts to restore the business lost owing to the uncertainty surrounding the sale of the Gardens. Some heats for the "Come Dancing" TV series were held in the Cumberland Suite, an under-18s disco was held on Thursday nights and dancing for the over-30s took place on Fridays, when Phil Moss and his Orchestra transferred to Belle Vue from the City's New Century Hall. Despite these efforts, the Company was not successful, being partly hampered by the condition of the rest of the site. GCS Ltd was declared bankrupt at the end of 1982.

The Exhibition Halls and suites were then sold by Espley Tyas to a new company called Mullet Ltd, which operated them as the New Belle Vue Centre. This concern enjoyed some initial success and the Exhibition Halls filled the gap pending the opening of G-MEX in March 1986. Mullet Ltd also dusted off the old plans for the refurbishment of the halls and provided a new common entrance off Redgate Lane at a total cost of about £200,000. The suites continued to be used for the dancing sessions, together with boxing organised by Belle Vue Promotions and the occasional wrestling match.

The sale of the Exhibition Halls and the suites by Espley Tyas was a sign that all was not well with their plans for the site. No taker could be found for the leisure centre that had featured so prominently in the original planning application. Nor could tenants be found for the proposed industrial and retail units, and none was built on a speculative basis. The reason for this apparent lack of interest was partly the declaration of a new Enterprise Zone in the nearby Salford Docks and Trafford Park area, where industrialists could enjoy rate-free periods of up to ten years. Faced with this, Espley Tyas's publicity for Belle Vue, which featured the slogan, "a future as bright as its past", proved to be ineffective and the Company considered other ways of recouping its investment in the site.

In February 1983 an application was submitted for a further four acres of housing fronting Hyde Road, and the same month the site was sold to McAlpine's for a development of forty-four houses known as Chantry Court. As with the earlier Wimpey scheme, sales on this site were very slow, only five being completed by February 1985, and building work halted shortly afterwards. In March 1984 a small area of land adjacent to Kirkmanshulme Lane was sold to Wolverhampton & Dudley Brewery Co for the erection of a new public house to replace the Longsight. The new pub opened on 3rd April 1985 and its lounges contain appropriate photographic reminders of the old Belle Vue. The old Longsight and the remaining parts of the 1851 entrance gateway were demolished in the first week of the following June. In October 1984 the last of the undeveloped land at the junction of Kirkmanshulme Lane and Redgate Lane was bought by the North Wales housebuilders, Redrow. Work on their housing scheme, Woodlands, began in late 1984 on the land which had originally been destined for industrial use by Espley Tyas. Unlike the two earlier housing schemes, sales were encouraging and the development was completed by late 1986. Following the demise of Espley Tyas (or Espley Trust, as it had become) in early 1985, the last remaining part of the Espley holding was sold to Canberra Developments. They proposed to erect small commercial units between Chantry Court and the Speedway Stadium, but there was little interest and none were built.

After the last Christmas Circus in the Kings Hall, efforts were made to maintain the tradition on the site for a few years. Roberts Brothers held a circus in the Speedway Stadium in 1982/83, repeating it on the Exhibition Hall car park the following year. In 1984/85 the

The Longsight Entrance gateway and pub being demolished in June 1985

show was put on by the Hoffman Circus on the Hyde Road car park. This lasted only three weeks, after which the site was handed over for the building of a large Roy Hall Cash & Carry store. The 1985/86 circus, also by Hoffman, took place on the Redgate Lane car park and was the final circus at the Belle Vue site.

1982 to 1987 was a period of mixed fortunes for the main Belle Vue site, with some schemes succeeding and others enjoying only initial success or none at all. The fate of the Belle Vue site was finally settled in 1987, with the inception of two large development schemes.

In a series of transactions, the British Car Auction Group assembled a large site comprising the undeveloped Canberra site together with the Speedway Stadium and the Exhibition Halls/Suites. (Stuart Bamforth had bought the latter from Mullet Ltd in mid 1987.) Although exhibitions had continued at Belle Vue after the opening of G-MEX, business must have declined. Bamforth initially had ideas of using the site of one of the halls to provide space for much needed improvements to the Stadium. However, in 1987 there was the prospect of legislation (after the tragic fire at Bradford football ground) which would have obliged Bamforth to invest heavily in ground safety measures - particularly onerous in the case of a wooden stadium like Belle Vue. This factor, no doubt together with the receipt of an offer "he could not refuse" from the BCA Group, caused him to sell the Stadium in autumn 1987. The final event there was a Stock Car meeting on 14th November. The Aces were disbanded, much to the dismay of fans, although fortunately only for a time, as by April 1988 they had been re-formed through the intervention of former star rider Peter Collins. They now ride at the Greyhound Stadium, their original 1928 home. This was adapted for their use following the receipt of a cash donation from the BCA Group. Shortly after November 1987 the Speedway Stadium was demolished and the BCA scheme built. The operation is now part of the ADT Car Auction Group. The restaurant within the main building has mementoes of Belle Vue's former years.

The other major development was the building of the Cannon "Showcase" Cinema, an American-style Multiplex with acres of car parking. This scheme, completed in 1989, effectively used up all the surplus land from the Wimpey and McAlpine housing sites. Outside the main Belle Vue site, the Greyhound Stadium continues to function and it, too, has had a certain revival of fortune in recent years. Apart from the adaptations to allow use by the Aces, it has had the benefit of a £1½ million improvement scheme over the last two years. The Aces continue to ride there, although their existence is said at times to have been financially precarious, and Peter Collins is no longer involved. On the adjoining Ducie High School site, formerly the Firework Land of the Jennison era, the City Council has redeveloped the school into a regional standard athletic facility, much appreciated in the area, which the Council has described as "continuing the traditional role of Belle Vue as a focal point for leisure activities in the City".

So what, today, is left of the old Belle Vue? Very little, in fact. From the Jennison era, only the Belle Vue Place houses, the Norman Street houses, the derelict Lake Hotel and the two off-site pubs, the Midland and the Garibaldi still stand. A short stretch of the tree-lined Avenue remains at the eastern end of the ADT site. From later eras, only the Greyhound Stadium and the Bowling Centre survive, and these were only semi-related to Belle Vue.

Away from Belle Vue itself, Maharajah can still be seen at the Manchester Museum. His life story is the subject of a very interesting book by David Barnaby. Heywood Hardy's painting, "The Disputed Toll", has been on display in the Manchester City Art Gallery since 1990. The September Brass Band Contests continue in the Free Trade Hall and the Brass Band Registry is located over a shop on the north side of Hyde Road, opposite the site of the former entrance to Belle Vue. The four steam locomotives from the Miniature Railway still exist and a few ex-Belle Vue animals can be seen by those who know where to find them. The Gorton Philharmonic perform in Stockport and elsewhere. Finally, Chetham's Library and the Manchester Central Reference Library have large collections of very interesting Belle Vue material.

The "new" Belle Vue comprises housing, a Multiplex cinema and a large car auction centre. It looks as though it will remain that way for a long time.

The derelict Lake Hotel in 1992, with the site advertised for sale

IN RETROSPECT

George Jennison, when writing his history of Belle Vue under the family in 1929, foresaw a time when the institution would be no more than a faded memory. Fortunately this is not yet the case, for although Belle Vue is no more, its demise is in the recent past and certain features such as the Speedway, greyhound racing and the Bowling Centre continue to function. In addition, "Belle Vue" has become established as the name of the district of Manchester surrounding the former Gardens.

However, as the years pass and the site slowly subsides under a sea of housing and other development, memories of Belle Vue Gardens will diminish, surviving records will become harder to trace and former members of staff will be fewer in number, making the work of the future historian that much more difficult. Hence the importance of presenting a reasonably definitive history of Belle Vue now.

What is the historical significance of Belle Vue and what should we remember it for? Before it closed, Belle Vue was the third oldest zoological gardens in the UK, after London and Bristol, and the first to be successfully operated by a commercial concern. Its doors were opened to the general public over ten years before Regent's Park and it was developed and run for nearly one hundred years by the same family, the Jennisons, who ensured that Belle Vue outlived all its competitors. The Zoo rapidly became the country's premier provincial zoo, a position it retained until the 1960s. Despite Belle Vue's commercial nature, the Zoo was a pioneer in introducing progressive methods of animal welfare, especially the provision of outdoor enclosures and the care of animals during winter. It had a consistently impressive record of breeding and animal longevity.

ZOOLOGICAL GARDENS, BELLE VUE.

ATTRACTIONS OF THE GARDENS:

Danson and Son's Colossal Open-air PICTURE of the

IMPERIAL CITY OF CALCUTTA,

Capital of the British Empire in India.

EVERY EVENING AT DUSK WILL BE REPRESENTED THE

FETES AND ILLUMINATIONS AT CALCUTTA

Upon the occasion of His Royal Highness the Prince of Wales's Visit to India,

WITH A MOST BRILLIANT DISPLAY OF FIREWORKS.

The Gardens, which are upwards of 45 acres in extent, contain large Conservatories, Ferneries, Two Mazes, &c. Pleasure Boats and Steamers will Ply on the Large Lakes as usual.

EXTENSIVE ZOOLOGICAL COLLECTION,

Including Lions, Tigers, Elephants, Giraffes, Polar & Russian Bears, Monkeys, Eagles, &c.

THREE BANDS on WHIT-FRIDAY, SATURDAY, and MONDAY after WHIT-WEEK, from Two p.m.

Admission: SIXPENCE. After Four, ONE SHILLING.

Advertisement from June 1876

Among Belle Vue's breeding "firsts" were the Indian cobras in 1931, 1932 and 1933 by James Craythorne, and this was repeated by his son Albert in 1953. Their successor, Clive Bennett, bred the Royal python in the Reptile House in 1972 and almost succeeded with the American alligator in the 1960s. Other breeding achievements included Ankole cattle, the Spekes sitatunga, or marsh buck, and the Beisa oryx (for the first time in the UK since 1881), all in the 1950s, and the kinkajou in the early 1960s. There were many examples of animal longevity. The American bison, in particular, lived thirty-six years, the record for this species in the UK.

The Zoo was home to unusual and rare animals on many occasions. Apart from the tigons and gerenuks already mentioned, the rare Indian rhino was kept by the Jennisons early this century, and both a hybrid sealion and a hybrid bear (a cross between a polar bear and a Kodiak bear) were also kept by them. In 1947 the Zoo acquired the very unusual Mexican bearded lizard, the first time such an animal had been seen in the country. The Komodo monitor lizard, commonly known as the Komodo dragon, and the tuatara were kept in the 1920s. These two animals were not seen anywhere else outside London. The unusual Banda sea snakes were kept later.

Belle Vue was famous for many other activities. The fireworks displays and brass band contests became well known regionally and nationally. The former outlasted all its imitators and kept going well into the twentieth century, while the latter continue to this day, albeit not at Belle Vue. The Amusement Park was the largest inland amusement park in the UK. Apart from the musical contests, the Kings Hall saw the Christmas Circus, political gatherings, religious meetings, orchestral celebrity and pop concerts. The Circus and the Speedway were the only ones to operate throughout the Second World War. The latter, established in the first large, purpose-built stadium for the sport in the country, hosted a team whose early years of success have not been equalled since. For a long time, the Belle Vue Exhibition Halls were the largest outside London and if the negotiations with the Corporation had been successful, Manchester would have pre-empted the facilities provided by Birmingham's National Exhibition Centre by some twenty years.

There is not space here to deal adequately with the reminiscences of staff and public. There are those who can recall the late Jennison era, with its watercress teas and outdoor dancing, and those of a later generation who enjoyed the thrill of the Bobs or Scenic Railway. Common to all such reminiscences is the sheer pleasure of the occasion of a visit to Belle Vue. Children anxiously ticked off the days leading up to their promised trip and once behind the forbidding perimeter walls they were in a completely different world - perhaps the nearest that Britain has achieved to America's Disneyland.

An institution like Belle Vue tended both to attract and to create its own characters. The Jennisons, the Iles's, George Lockhart and others deserve biographies of their own. The contribution of lower-level employees cannot be overlooked. Belle Vue Zoo's excellent reputation owes much to its staff, who proved that good animal welfare depends not just on physical facilities and good veterinary work, but also on care, dedication and practical knowledge which can only be built up over a lifetime of experience.

Employment at Belle Vue was often a family affair, with fathers being followed by sons, especially in the Zoo. Despite the low wages paid throughout the Gardens, and the long and inconvenient hours, many former members of staff and management recall with fondness their days at Belle Vue, and look back on their years spent in the Gardens as the most fulfilling and enjoyable of their entire careers, even though many went on to more lucrative posts.

Need Belle Vue have closed? On commercial grounds, this was probably inevitable, although there are many who would seek to criticise some of the decisions taken in the last years of operation by its owners and managers. Since its passing, Manchester has been deprived of a substantial leisure facility within its boundaries, and the conurbation is the only one not possessing a major zoo. Despite the much talked about demise of the urban zoo, Belle Vue is still the only large zoo to have closed its doors, although at time of writing (1991) the future of London Zoo is in the balance.

Lorenzo Lawrence, who came to Belle Vue with Maharajah in 1872 and remained as Elephant Keeper for over forty years

The only way that Belle Vue could have been saved would have been through public assistance of one form or another. Unfortunately this was not forthcoming at the right time, although many will wonder at the true purpose of a planning system which allows the representations of fifty thousand petitioners to be ignored. Had such assistance been forthcoming, Belle Vue would have celebrated its 150th anniversary in 1986.

Beisa oryx in the Rocky Mountain Enclosure, late 1940s

Whatever one thinks of these things, one cannot help concluding that a great opportunity to save something worthwhile was very narrowly missed, and that the end of Belle Vue as it was will, in the course of time, be very deeply regretted.

In 1888, a contributor to "Manchester of Today" wrote:

"Deprived of her magnificent zoological gardens, Manchester would...have passed into some new and undesirable sphere of existence to nine-tenths of her great population, and would have lost her chief attraction to the vast community of annual visitors and migratory sightseers with which the metropolis of the cotton trade...is not unpleasantly familiar."